Windows ® *95*

Timothy J. O'Leary
Linda I. O'Leary

8 9 0 BAN BAN 9 0 9 8

ISBN 0-07-049054-6

Library of Congress Catalog Card Number 95-77491

Credits: Page WN2, Figure 1 courtesy of Gateway 2000; page WN5, Figure 3 courtesy of Microsoft Corp.; page WN5, Figure 4 courtesy of Intel; page WN10, Figure 7 (inset) courtesy of Hewlett-Packard.

Contents

Introduction to the Windows 95 Labs

Each lab module in the *McGraw-Hill Microcomputing* series consists of a sequence of labs that each require about one hour to complete. They are designed to provide you with practical skills in using the following kinds of software, which are the most widely used in business and industry:

- Windows 95
- Word processor
- Spreadsheet
- Database
- Graphics presentation

The labs describe not only the most important commands and concepts, but also explain why and under what circumstances you will use them. By presenting an ongoing case study based on input from actual business managers, we show how such software is used in a real business setting.

Organization of the Lab Modules

The Lab Modules Are Organized in the Following Categories: Overview, Labs, Case Project, Glossary of Key Terms, Functional Summary of Selected Commands, Windows 95 Review, and Index.

Overview   The overview, which appears at the beginning of each module, describes (1) what the program can do for you, (2) what the program is, (3) the generic terms that this and all similar programs use (for example, all word processing programs, regardless of brand name), and (4) the case study to be presented in the module for that program. The overview also includes a Before You Begin section that presents information for both students and instructors about hardware and software settings and other items of importance to be considered before beginning the labs.

WNiii

Labs   The labs consist of both concept coverage and detailed, step-by-step directions for completing the problem presented in the case. The concepts appear in folder-like boxes preceding the step-by-step directions on how to apply the concept. Your progress through the labs is reinforced by the use of carefully placed figures that represent how your screen should appear after you complete a procedure. Labs should be followed in sequence, because each succeeding lab builds on the one preceding it. In addition, as you progress through the labs, the number of screen displays decreases and directions become less specific. This feature allows you to think about what you have learned, avoids simple rote learning, and reinforces earlier concepts and commands, helping you to gain confidence.

In case there is not enough lab time to complete the entire lab, the labs are often divided into two parts. When needed, instructions about how to end Part 1 and begin Part 2 appear at the end of Part 1.

Case Project   Many lab modules include a complex project that allows you to apply and integrate the concepts you have learned throughout the labs.

Glossary of Key Terms   The glossary, which appears at the end of each lab module, defines all the key terms that appear in bold in the overview and throughout the labs.

Functional Summary of Selected Commands   Each lab module includes a quick-reference source for selected commands. The commands are listed in the order in which they appear in the application's menu.

Windows 95 Review   A brief review of Windows 95 features and concepts is included as an appendix to assist students who need help with basic Windows 95 features.

Index   Each lab module contains an index for quick reference to specific items within that module.

Organization of the Labs

The Labs Consist of the Following Parts: Competencies, Concept Overview, Case Study, Lab Review, Hands-On Practice Exercises, and Concept Summary.

Competencies   The competencies list appears at the beginning of each lab. It lists the concepts and commands to be learned in that particular lab.

Concept Overview   Throughout the labs, the major concepts appear in folder-like boxes. The concept overview at the beginning of each lab provides a brief introduction to those concepts. They are in numbered order as presented in the lab.

Case Study   The ongoing case study shows how to solve real-world business problems using the application covered by that particular module. The ongoing case study was written with the help of real-world experience contributed by industry managers. The specific case study used in each lab module is explained in the overview section for the module. The reader follows the instructions in the labs to solve the case problems.

Lab Review　The Lab Review includes a summary of terms and commands, as well as a variety of exercises designed to reinforce concepts and procedures presented in the lab. The review exercises do not require the use of a computer. The Lab Review consists of the following elements:

- *Key Terms*　Terms that are defined in the labs appear in **boldface** type. They are also listed at the end of each lab in alphabetical order. The number of the page on which the term is introduced follows the term.

- *Command Summary*　All commands that are used in the lab and the actions they perform are listed at the end of each lab in the order in which they appear on menus. The Command Summary also includes keyboard and toolbar shortcuts.

- *Matching*　A variety of different types of matching problems is presented. The matching problems emphasize both concepts and procedures through the use of traditional matching and identification exercises and action/result–type matching exercises.

- *Fill-In Questions*　The ten fill-in questions are designed to reinforce concepts presented in the lab.

Hands-On Practice Exercises　Each lab also includes a Hands-On Practice Exercises section that requires the use of a computer to complete. This section is divided into two areas: Step by Step and On Your Own. The Step by Step exercises lead the student through the steps needed to complete the problem. The On Your Own exercises provide limited directions. Each exercise is marked with stars that indicate the difficulty level of the problem. The star rating system is: *Easy, **Moderate, ***Difficult. Each section includes problems having a variety of levels of difficulty.

Concept Summary　The final item that appears at the end of each lab is the Concept Summary. This two-page spread presents a visual summary of the concepts presented in the lab.

Procedural Conventions

Commands and Directions Are Expressed Through Certain Standard Conventions.

We have followed certain conventions in the labs for indicating keys, key combinations, commands, command sequences, and other directions.

Keys   Computer keys are expressed in abbreviated form, as follows:

Computer Keys	Display in Text
Alternate	Alt
Backspace	←Backspace
Caps Lock (Capital Lock)	Caps Lock
Ctrl (Control)	Ctrl
Del (Delete)	Del
End	End
ESC (Escape)	Esc
(Enter/Return)	←Enter
Home	Home
Ins (Insert)	Ins
Num Lock (Number Lock)	Num Lock
Pg Dn (Page Down)	Page Down
Pg Up (Page Up)	Page Up
Prt Sc (Print Screen)	Prt Sc
Scroll Lock	Scroll Lock
Shift	⇧Shift
Tab	Tab ↹
Function Keys	
F1 through F12	F1 through F12
Cursor Movement	
↑ (Up)	↑
↓ (Down)	↓
← (Left)	←
→ (Right)	→

Key Combinations   Many programs require that you use a combination of keys for a particular command (for example, the pair of keys Ctrl and F4). You should press them in the order in which they appear, from left to right, holding down the first key while pressing the second. In the labs, commands that are used in this manner are separated by a plus—for example, Ctrl + F4 .

Directions   The principal directions in the labs are "Press," "Move to," "Type," "Choose," "Select," and "Click." These directions appear on a separate line beginning at the left margin, as follows:

■ *Press:* This means you should strike a key. Usually a command key will follow the direction (such as Delete for "Delete"). For example:

Press: Delete

■ *Move to:* This means you should move the insertion point or highlight to the location indicated. For example, the direction to move to cell A5 would appear as:

Move to: A5

■ *Type:* This means you should type or key in certain letters or numbers, just as you would on a typewriter keyboard. Whatever is to be typed will appear in bright blue type. For example:

Type: January

■ *Choose and Select:* A sequence of selections from a menu or dialog box is often required to complete a command. The selections are made using the mouse or keyboard. The command sequences will follow the word "Choose." If a letter of a command appears with an underline and in **boldface**, you can select that command by typing the letter. The command sequence that is to be typed will appear in bright blue.

"Select" is used to indicate selecting or marking an item from a list of available options. "Select" does not begin an action as "Choose" does. Selecting may be part of a command sequence and will usually appear when procedures are initially introduced. In the beginning these commands are introduced separately. For example:

Choose: File
Select: Open
Select: MEMBERS.DOC
Choose: OK

Later, as you become more familiar with the program, the commands are combined on a single line. Each command may be separated by a /. For example,

Choose: File/Open/MEMBERS.DOC/OK

■ *Click:* If a command procedure has a mouse shortcut, the mouse shortcut is preceded with the word "Click." (The menu equivalent or keyboard shortcut appears as a marginal note.) For example:

Click: **B** Bold

Additional directions may appear as bright blue text embedded within the main text. They appear like this only after the procedure to perform the directions is very familiar to the student. Follow the directions using the appropriate procedure.

Marginal Notes Throughout the labs notes appear in the margins. These notes may be reminders of how to perform a procedure, clarifications or alternate methods, or brief side notes that expand upon a concept. The marginal notes symbols have different meanings as illustrated below:

A standard informational note:

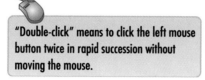

The menu equivalent is Format/Font/Bold and the keyboard shortcut is Ctrl + B.

An informational note for mouse users:

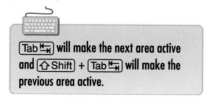

"Double-click" means to click the left mouse button twice in rapid succession without moving the mouse.

A note for keyboard users:

Tab will make the next area active and ⇧ Shift + Tab will make the previous area active.

A note that refers the reader to information in the Overview:

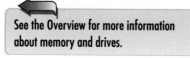

See the Overview for more information about memory and drives.

A note that refers readers to information in the Windows 95 Review:

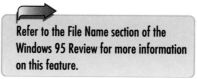

Refer to the File Name section of the Windows 95 Review for more information on this feature.

A warning note:

> **WARNING!**
> To avoid damaging files, always shut down Windows before you turn off your computer.

General System Requirements

To complete the labs, the following hardware and software are needed:

- An IBM or IBM-compatible computer system with a hard disk and one or two floppy disk drives. The amount of RAM memory your computer must have varies with the application software program you will be using. If you are using a networked system, your instructor will provide additional instructions as needed.

- A mouse. Mouse use is assumed, although keyboard directions are provided as marginal notes.

- A printer.

- Windows 95 and the application software programs selected by your instructor and installed on your computer.

- Student data disk containing the files needed to perform the labs and to complete the hands-on practice exercises; these files are supplied by your instructor.

Special Assumptions   Any special directions or hardware and software assumptions that have been made in the preparation of these lab modules are described at the end of the overview for that particular software application module under the heading "Before You Begin."

Supplements

Each Lab Module Is Accompanied by the Following Supplements:

- **Teaching Materials**   The Instructors Manual provides lecture notes and guidelines for the instructor on the concepts and procedures presented in each lab. It also includes the answers to all lab review problems and hands-on practice exercises, as well as for the case project. In addition, a copy of the test bank questions and the test answer key is supplied.

- **Transparency Masters**   Illustrations and screen shots that can be used to demonstrate concepts and procedures are provided as transparency masters.

■   **Electronic Transparencies**   The illustrations and screen shots that are included as transparency masters are also available in electronic form as PowerPoint slides.

■   **Computerized Test Bank**   A minimum of 40 true/false and multiple choice–type questions is supplied for each lab. With the MicroTest III Computerized Test Bank, instructors can network a test in the lab, give students a test on disk, and prepare traditional pencil-and-paper tests. It also allows full editing of individual test items.

■   **Data Disk**   The files that are required to complete the labs and hands-on practice exercises are provided on the data disk that is supplied with the teaching materials. Answers to all lab exercises are also included.

Windows 95 Overview

GETTING STARTED WITH YOUR MICROCOMPUTER

A microcomputer system is composed of five essential parts: people, procedures, software, hardware, and data. The end users (people) need to know how to operate the computer hardware and use the software programs to input and analyze data or information. To learn how to operate or use the software, hardware, and data, the end users follow procedures. Procedures consist of rules or guidelines to follow that are described in manuals. This overview will focus briefly on the hardware and software aspects of your computer system.

Computer Hardware

The physical part of the computer system, called **hardware**, consists of four parts: input devices, the system unit, secondary storage devices, and output devices.

The **input devices** take data and programs and put them into a form the computer can process. The most common input devices are a keyboard and a mouse. The **system unit** is the electronic circuitry housed within the computer cabinet. It holds the computer's **memory** and the **central processing unit** (CPU). The system unit executes programs, performs calculations, and temporarily stores data and programs. The most common form of **secondary storage** is a disk. It provides a place to permanently store information or data that is input into the computer. **Output devices** are pieces of equipment that translate the processed information from the CPU into a form that you can understand. A computer screen or monitor is the most common output device. It displays your work while you are using the computer. A printer is used to create printed output. In addition, speakers are becoming common sound output devices on many systems. A typical computer system is shown in Figure 1.

Figure 1

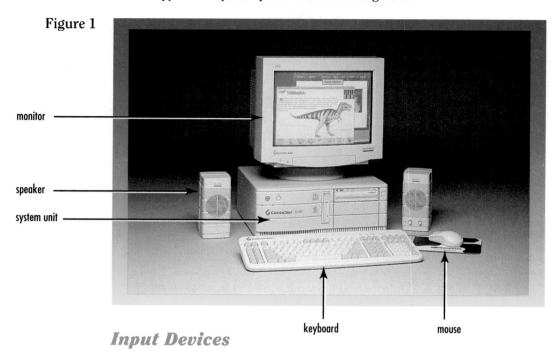

monitor

speaker

system unit

keyboard

mouse

Input Devices

Keyboard The **keyboard** is the most common type of input device. It allows you to communicate with the computer. It consists of four main areas: the function keys, the typewriter keys, the numeric keypad, and special-purpose keys. Two styles of keyboards are commonly found: the standard keyboard and the enhanced keyboard. Figure 2 shows a standard and an enhanced IBM keyboard.

Figure 2

Enhanced Keyboard

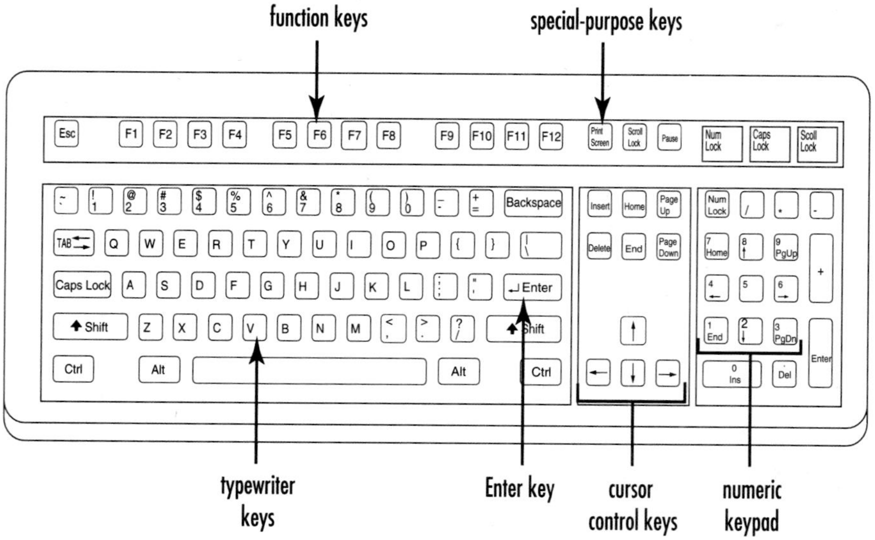

function keys

special-purpose keys

typewriter
keys

Enter key

cursor
control keys

numeric
keypad

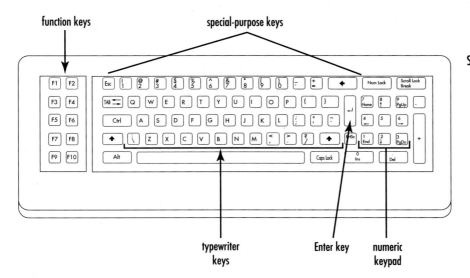

function keys

special-purpose keys

Standard Keyboard

typewriter
keys

Enter key

numeric
keypad

The central area of the keyboard contains the standard typing keys and the spacebar. The standard keys consist of letters, numbers, and special characters such as the semicolon and the dollar sign, as they appear on a standard typewriter. You use these keys just like you would a normal typewriter. As you type, the characters appear on the computer screen rather than on paper. The **cursor**, also called the **insertion point**, is a flashing bar that identifies your location on the screen.

The other typing keys and their uses are described below.

Key	Action
⇧Shift + letter	Types uppercase letter
⇧Shift + number	Types symbol shown above number on that key
Caps Lock	Allows entry of all uppercase alphabetic characters without using ⇧Shift
Tab	Moves insertion point preset number of spaces to the right
⇧Shift + Tab	Moves insertion point preset number of spaces to the left
←Enter	Moves the insertion point to the next line (same as a typewriter); allows the user to enter data or command sequences

At the right side of the keyboard is the numeric keypad. It consists of nine keys with arrows and numbers on them. These keys can be used to enter numbers or to direct the movement of the insertion point on the screen. To use the numeric keypad to enter numbers, the Num Lock key must be on. To turn on Num Lock, press the Num Lock key. When Num Lock is on, the indicator light on an enhanced keyboard is lighted. When Num Lock is off, use of the keys in the numeric keypad moves the insertion point in the direction of the arrow. The Num Lock key acts like a toggle switch to switch control of the numeric keypad between numeric entry and insertion point movement. On the enhanced keyboard there is a separate directional keypad consisting of four arrow keys that are used exclusively to move the insertion point.

There are also some keys in the numeric keypad with words on them: Home, End, Page Up, and Page Down. These keys will have different meanings depending on the software program you are using. You can use these keys to quickly move around information on your screen.

Function keys are located across the top on the enhanced keyboard or on the left side of standard keyboards. They are labeled F1, F2, etc. They are used to send instructions to the software being used. Therefore, their use varies with the software program you are using. Frequently, function keys are short-cuts for a long command. For example, instead of having to press several keys to perform a command, all you need to do is press one function key.

Scattered throughout the keyboard are special-purpose keys. The uses of these keys change with the type of work you are doing. Generally they have the following uses:

Key	Action
Esc (escape)	Quits or goes back one step in a program command; erases existing command
Ctrl (control)	Used in combination with another key to perform a special task
Alt (alternate)	Assigns another function to a given key
Print Screen	Prints a hard copy of whatever is on the screen (on standard keyboards you must hold down ⇧Shift in conjunction with Print Screen).
Scroll Lock	When on, using the ↑ and ↓ keys moves document up or down on the screen, and insertion point does not move
Pause	May let you stop a program for a short time
Break	Stops a command from completing execution
Insert and Ins	Allows you to insert characters between other characters
Delete and Del	Erases character insertion point is on
Backspace	Moves insertion point to left and erases character (this key may also appear as a left-facing arrow ←).
End, Home, Page Up, Page Down	Same effect as their equivalents on numeric keypad

Mouse   The mouse is an input device that is used in addition to the keyboard. It is a hand-held device that controls a pointer on the screen. When you move the mouse around the desktop, the rubber-coated ball on the bottom of the mouse moves. The ball's movement is translated into signals that tell the computer how to move the onscreen pointer. On top of the mouse are two buttons that are used to make selections from items on the screen.

Figure 3

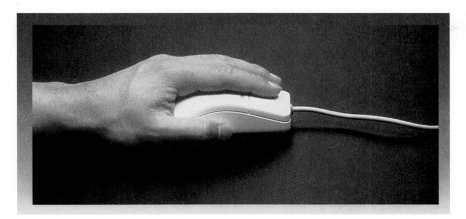

The System Unit

The system unit contains the central processing unit (CPU) and memory. Figure 4 displays the parts of a system unit.

Figure 4

RAM

ROM

microprocessor

The **central processing unit (CPU)** is the part of the computer system that does the actual computing. It contains the electronic circuitry through which data is processed and instructions are executed. In a microcomputer, the CPU consists of a single silicon chip, called a **microprocessor**, such as the model shown in Figure 4 made by Intel Corporation.

Memory, also called **primary storage**, is where data and instructions are stored during processing by the microprocessor. There are two types of memory, **read-only memory (ROM)** and **random-access memory (RAM)** (see Figure 4). The ROM chips contain programs that are built into the chips and direct the operations of the computer. ROM is not accessible to the user. The other type of memory, RAM, is accessible to the user. It is the computer's workplace. The RAM chips hold the software programs and data that the CPU is currently processing. RAM is also referred to as **temporary memory** because whatever is in RAM is lost if the power is turned off.

Memory is located in the system unit on tiny memory chips. Depending on the amount of memory your computer system has, the number of chips will vary. The amount of memory is measured in **bytes**. A byte is a single memory location. Usually a byte stores one character. A **kilobyte (KB)** equals 1024 (or approximately 1000) bytes. A **megabyte (MB)** holds approximately 1 million bytes, and a **gigabyte (GB)** holds approximately 1 billion bytes. Most microcomputer systems sold today have a memory capacity of 8MB or more.

Secondary Storage

Secondary storage devices provide a means of permanently storing the information contained in temporary memory. There are several types of secondary storage devices. The most common type of secondary storage is a **disk**. The disk is the permanent storage medium for either data (for example, a business letter) or a software program (for example, a word processor to edit that letter). The data and program information are stored on circular metal or plastic disks as a series of electromagnetic spots. The disk can be an internal **hard disk** that is housed within the system unit, or an external **floppy disk**. In addition, the **CD-ROM disk** is another type of secondary storage device commonly found in computer systems sold today. This type of disk is an optical disk that uses a laser beam to alter the surface of the disk to store data

The amount of data a disk can hold is called **disk capacity**. Disk capacity, like memory, is measured in kilobytes, megabytes, and gigabytes.

Hard Disk The hard disk is a permanent fixture containing one or more circular metallic disks that are used to store data files and software programs. The internal hard disk is sealed in a container to prevent any foreign matter from getting inside. Most microcomputer systems sold today have a hard disk capacity of at least 540MB.

The **hard-disk drive** in the system unit provides the means for you to retrieve and save your data and programs onto the hard disk. This disk drive contains an access arm and read-write heads for writing data to and reading data from the disk. It is usually referred to as the C drive.

The main advantages of a hard disk are that more information can be stored on it, and it is more quickly accessed than the information from a floppy disk.

Floppy Disk The second main type of secondary storage is the floppy disk. Floppy disks store data on a flexible plastic disk. It allows the user to load instructions into the computer from disks containing software programs and to save data onto and retrieve data from disks that contain information you create. The main advantage of floppy disks is that they are transportable.

Floppy disks come in several sizes. The most common sizes are 5.25 inches and 3.5 inches. The 3.5-inch disk is the most common disk used today. The type of disk you use will depend on your computer hardware requirements. Figure 5 shows the 3.5-inch disk.

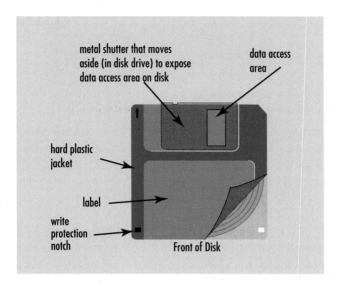

Figure 5

The 3.5-inch disks are contained within a hard plastic jacket that protects the disk. Inside the hard jacket is the soft plastic disk that is used to store the data. The write-protect notch is covered by a sliding shutter. When the shutter is open, the write-protect hole is exposed, preventing information from being changed on the disk.

A **floppy-disk drive** is used to read information from the floppy-disk to RAM and write information from RAM to the disk. The floppy disk drive also has an access arm and read-write heads. All microcomputers have at least one floppy-disk drive.

The floppy-disk drive is housed in the front of the computer as shown in Figure 5. A slot allows you to insert a floppy disk into the drive. The data is read from or written to the disk by the read-write head mechanism inside each drive.

If there are two disk drives, they are referred to as the A drive and the B drive. If the drives are positioned side by side, generally the A drive is on the left. If your drives are located one above the other, the A drive is the one on top.

The capacity of floppy disks varies with the type of disk, from 360KB up to 2.88MB. Several factors control how much data can be stored on a floppy disk. If the disk is a single-sided disk, data can be stored on one side of the disk only. Double-sided disks store data on both sides of the disk. Most disks are double-sided disks. Another factor that affects the amount of data that can be stored on a disk is whether the disk is a single-density, double-density, or high-density disk. Density refers to the number of bytes that can be recorded on the disk in a specified space. The higher density the disk is, the more data that can be stored. The chart below summarizes the different types and capacities of floppy disks.

Diameter (inches)	Description (bytes)	Capacity
5.25	Double-sided, high-density	1.25MB
3.5	Double-sided, double-density	720KB
3.5	Double-sided, high-density	1.44MB

It is important to be aware of the density of disks because the disk drive on your computer must be able to support the disk capacity of the disk, or it will be unable to use the disk. A higher density drive can read from and write to a lower density disk, but a lower density drive cannot read from or write to a higher density disk.

Floppy Disk Care Since floppy disks contain a permanent copy of your work or program files that you use frequently, it is very important that this data not be lost or destroyed. If it is, you could lose a lot of time and effort. To help preserve your disks, there are some things you should know about their care and handling:

1. Excessive heat can melt or warp the disk. Do not, for example, expose your disk to excessive sunlight through the window of your car or to excessive heat by placing it on your heater.

2. Disks use magnetism to store your data. Do not expose the disk to magnetic fields such as your telephone receiver, a loudspeaker, or a television. The magnetic fields from these machines can alter the data on your disk.

3. Do not touch the surface of the plastic disk. Always handle the case only. The oils from your skin can damage the surface of the disk.

In addition, if you are using 5.25-inch disks, the following precautions should be taken:

1. Store your disks standing up or in a vertical position. This way they will not bend or warp. Always place the 5.25-disk in its protective envelope.

2. Do not bend disks or place heavy objects on them.

3. Do not write on a 5.25-inch disk with a ball-point pen. The pressure from the pen can crease the disk and damage it. If you must write on your disk, use a felt-tip pen. It is best, however, to write on the label before you place it on the disk.

CD-ROM Disks The third main type of secondary storage is the **CD-ROM disk**. CD-ROM stands for compact disk-read-only memory. Like compact disks you buy at a music store, a CD-ROM disk is a read-only disc. This means that it cannot be written on or erased by the user. Thus, you only have access to the information imprinted on the disk by the publisher. Figure 6 shows a CD-ROM and CD-ROM drive.

Figure 6

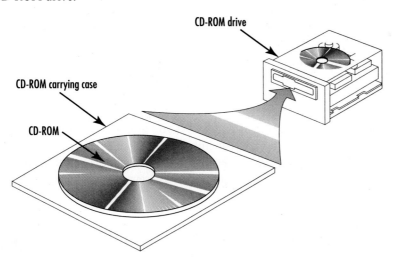

CD-ROM drive

CD-ROM carrying case

CD-ROM

A CD-ROM disk is created using a laser beam, which alters the surface of the disk, creating flat and bumpy areas called "pits" on the bottom of the disk. These areas represent data. A **CD-ROM drive** uses a laser that projects a tiny beam of light onto the disk to read the data.

A typical CD-ROM disk is 5.25 inches in diameter and can store 650MB of data, the equivalent of 147 floppy disks. Because of their large storage capacity, they are commonly used to distribute large databases and references, such as an encyclopedia. In addition, they are used to distribute large software programs and computer games.

Output Devices

The Computer Screen The computer screen, or **monitor**, is how the computer communicates with you. The monitor displays instructions you send to the computer and the information and results from the computer back to you. It relays program messages or instructions called prompts and displays results of calculations, graphs, and text input.

The computer screen can be either a monochrome screen display or a color screen display. A monochrome screen uses only one color—usually white, green, amber, or black—to display text on a contrasting background. Color screens commonly display 256 colors at once from a selection of over 256,000 choices.

The Printer Along with the computer screen, a **printer** serves as a way for the computer to tell you what you have input and what it has done. The difference is that the printer generates a permanent hard copy of your work on paper.

Some printers can print both text and graphics (pictures). Others can print only text. If you have a printer that prints only text, you would need a device called a **plotter** to print graphs. Printers can produce hard copy that is either near letter (draft) quality or letter quality. Draft-quality print is formed by a series of dots and consequently may not appear solid. Letter-quality print is solid, like that produced by a typewriter. Many printers can also produce color output.

Dot-matrix printers are often used to create draft-quality output. They produce letters by a series of pins that press on a printer ribbon to produce dots in the form of the letter. These printers are fast and economical, but noisy. Letter-quality print is commonly produced by ink-jet and laser printers. The ink-jet printer sprays ink in the pattern of the character. Ink-jet printers have recently become the most widely used type of printer. The laser printer creates characters by means of an electronic charge. The laser printer is a high-resolution printer that produces typeset-quality text and graphics. Figure 7 shows a laser printer and how it creates letter-quality text.

Although most printers can also print graphs, you may want to use a plotter to draw pictures and graphs. Most plotters use several pens of different colors to

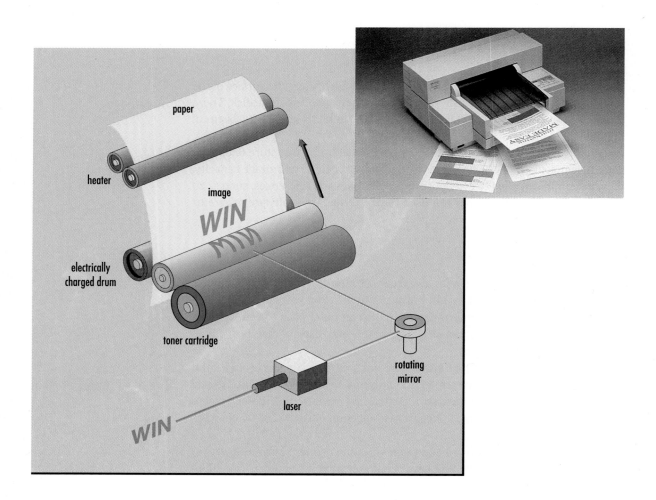

produce a multicolor drawing. The graphs and drawings produced by a plotter have much better line resolution and precision than graphs produced by a dot-matrix printer. A plotter produces professional presentation-quality graphs.

Computer Software

Software is the set of instructions that directs the computer to process information. These instructions are called **programs**. Without software, the computer cannot work. A commonly used analogy is that the computer hardware is the engine, while the software is the fuel that allows the engine to operate. Without software the hardware would be useless. There are two types of software available for computers: system software and application software.

System Software **System software** programs coordinate the operation of the various hardware components of the computer. The system software or operating system program helps the user to actually operate the computer system. They are an interface between the user and the computer.

The operating system oversees the processing of the application programs and all input and output of the system. Without the operating system, you cannot use the applications software programs provided with this book. The operating system controls computer system resources and coordinates the flow of data to and from the microprocessor and to and from input and output devices such as the keyboard and the monitor.

System software is usually provided by the computer manufacturer. The various types of computers require different types of system software programs in order to operate. Some of the most popular are DOS, Macintosh operating system, OS/2, Windows 95, and UNIX.

Application Software **Application software** is a set of programs designed for specific uses or "applications," such as word processing, graphics, or spreadsheet analysis. Application software can be custom-written but is usually purchased ready-made.

Normally, to use an application program like Excel 7.0, you load the program into the computer's memory; execute (run) the program; and then create, edit, or update a file. When you have finished, you need to save the work you have done on a disk. If you do not save your work and you turn off the computer, it is erased from memory and everything you have done will be lost.

The operating system acts as a communications link between the hardware and the application program. It is responsible for loading the application software into memory and then starting the program. It also retrieves data files and saves them to disk when directed. When you have finished using the application software you are returned to the operating system.

Before You Begin

We suggest that schools use the default Windows settings stored in the initial.ini file, and that this .ini file is copied over the .ini file that is saved on exiting

Windows. This way student changes will not be saved, and the same layout will be in effect each time Windows 95 is started.

Command sequences appear following the word "Choose." Multiple menu selections are separated with a /. If available, keyboard shortcuts will be presented in marginal notes. Alternative toolbar shortcuts for the command will appear following the word "Click." Any one of these methods can be used to enter the command.

We have also made the following assumptions:

- Data files are in separate folders for the different applications that will be used (Word 7.0, Excel 7.0, Windows 95, etc.) under the Student Data File folder on the hard drive.

- The Windows 95 supplemental applications Clipboard Viewer and Quick View have also been installed. To install these, use Add/Remove Programs from the Control Panel.

Windows 95 Basic Skills

Learning to use a computer is like any other skill. You start by learning the basic concepts and skills. Then you build upon these basics as you apply and expand your knowledge.

This lab marks the beginning in your pursuit of computer competency by introducing you to many of the basic features and concepts that are common to all Windows applications. At the same time you will learn about the Windows 95 operating system and how to use it to perform tasks you will need to use on a daily basis. This includes the ability to identify and use the parts of the desktop and a window. In addition, you will learn about other features such as using a mouse, moving and sizing windows, using menus and dialog boxes, accessing and using Help, and formatting a disk. These concepts are basic to all Windows applications and provide you with the skills you will need while learning to use all other Windows applications.

Concept Overview

The following concepts will be introduced in this lab:

1. What's Windows 95?   Windows 95 is an operating system program that uses a graphical interface to control all the parts of your computer.

2. The Desktop   The Windows 95 screen is called the desktop. It displays icons that represent various tools and features.

3. The Mouse   The mouse is a hand-held hardware device that is attached to your computer. It controls an arrow called a pointer that appears on your screen.

4. Menus   A menu is one of many methods used to tell a program what you want it to do. When opened, a menu displays a list of commands.

5. Help   The Windows Help facility is a quick source of information about commands or features.

6. Dialog Box   A dialog box is how Windows programs provide and request information from you in order to complete a task.

7. Scroll Bar   A scroll bar is used with a mouse to bring additional lines of information into view in a window or list box.

8. Window   A window is a rectangular section of the screen that is dedicated to a specific activity or application.

9. Moving Windows   Moving a window displays the window at another location on the desktop, making it easier to view other items.

10. Sizing Windows   A window can be changed to just about any size you want, making it easier to see more or less information in the window.

11. Formatting a Disk   Before a new disk can be used, you must format or convert it from a generic state into a format that can be used by your computer.

12. Status Bar   A status bar at the bottom of the window displays information about program settings you are using and the task being performed.

13. Properties   All items on the screen have settings and attributes, called properties, associated with them.

Part 1

Starting Windows 95

The **operating system** program controls computer system resources and coordinates the flow of data to and from the system unit and to and from input and output devices like the keyboard and the display screen. It allows you to create and manage files and run applications software programs. This series of labs will introduce you to the newest operating system, Windows 95.

OPERATING SYSTEM

Concept 1: What's Windows 95?

Windows 95 is an operating system program that controls all the parts of your computer. It uses a **graphical user interface** (GUI, pronounced "gooey"). This kind of interface displays graphical objects called **icons**, which represent the items you use. The icons are buttons that when "pushed" activate the item.

All programs that use the Windows operating system have a **common user interface** that makes it easy to learn and use different programs that run under Windows. A common user interface means that programs have common features, such as the same menu commands. For example, you will find the command to open a file is the same command in all Windows 95 applications.

The Windows operating system gets its name from its use of rectangular boxes called **windows** that are used to display information and other programs. Multiple windows can be open at the same time, making it easy to move from one task to another. This is how people work. More than likely you have several projects you are working on during the day, and need to be able to switch easily from one to the other.

Refer to the Overview for information about memory and drives.

How you proceed depends on whether your computer is on or off. Your computer is on if you can hear the fan running and, on many machines, lights are lit on the front. Otherwise, your computer is off.

If your computer is off, turning it on performs a memory check to determine whether all the memory locations are able to receive and store data correctly and initializes the equipment for use by accessing the disk drives and printer. This is called a **cold start**.

If your computer is on, you can restart the computer without turning the power switch off and on again. This is called a **warm start**. A warm start does not perform a memory check, but it does initialize the equipment for use.

Following either a cold or warm start, the Windows 95 files are automatically loaded into the main memory of your computer.

If your computer is off, follow the steps below:

1. Turn on the power switch. The power switch is commonly located on the back or right side of your computer. It may also be a button that you push on the front of your computer.

2. If necessary, turn your monitor on and adjust the contrast and brightness. Generally, the button to turn on the monitor is located on the front of the monitor. Use the dials (generally located in the panel on the front of the monitor) to adjust the monitor.

3. Continue the lab below the box on page 17.

If your computer is on, follow the steps below:

1. **If necessary, turn your monitor on and adjust the contrast and brightness.** Generally, the button to turn on the monitor is located on the front of the monitor. Use the dials (generally located in the panel on the front of the monitor) to adjust the monitor.

2. **If your screen looks like Figure 1-3 on page 20, Windows 95 is already started. Skip to the section "Exploring the Desktop" on page 19.**

3. **If your screen looks like Figure 1-2 on page 18, Windows 95 is already started. Skip to below Figure 1-2 to continue.**

4. **If your screen displays the box shown in Figure 1-1, you need to restart your computer following the directions below.**

Figure 1-1

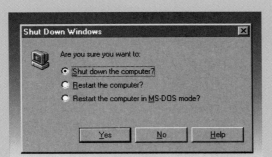

The box on your screen (shown in Figure 1-1) displays 3 (or 4 if your system is networked) choices or options. To select the option to restart the computer,

Type: R

A dot appears in the circle before this option, indicating that it is selected.
    Then, to confirm your selection, you need to choose "Yes." To do this,

Press: ⟵Enter

After a few moments, the Windows opening screen is displayed. This screen is quickly followed by the Windows 95 screen and a Welcome to Windows 95 box as shown in Figure 1-2.
    If your screen does not display the Welcome box, this feature has been turned off. If this is the case, skip to the section "Exploring the Desktop on page 19."
    The Welcome box displays a "Did you know" message that provides different short informational tips about Windows 95 each time the program is started.
    Read the "Did you know" message.

You can type lowercase or uppercase letters.

If you know how to use a mouse already, you can click on the Restart the Computer option to select it.

If you know how to use a mouse already, you can click on Yes to select it.

If a log-on prompt appears, type in your user name and password in the appropriate spaces and then press ⟵Enter (or click OK).

Figure 1-2

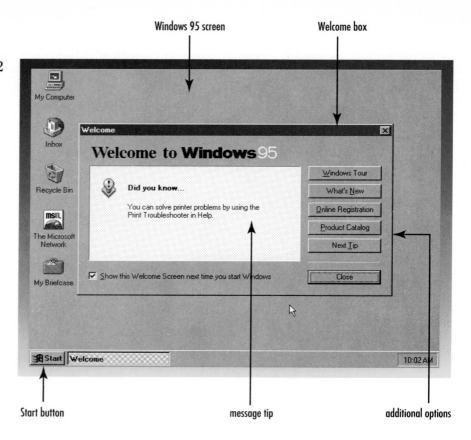

Windows 95 screen   Welcome box

Start button   message tip   additional options

In addition, the Welcome box includes several options that when selected access information about different features, such as the Windows Tour and a discussion of What's New in Windows 95. You will learn how to use this type of box later in the lab. For now, to close the box,

If you already know how to use a mouse, you can click Close.

Press: Esc

The Welcome box is closed, and your screen should be similar to Figure 1-3 on the page 20.

Exploring the Desktop

The screen displays the Windows desktop. It is called a desktop because it is similar to the way you might organize the work on your desk — a different place or pile of paper for each tool or related group of materials.

Concept 2: The Desktop

The Windows 95 screen is called a **desktop**. It displays icons that represent various tools and features. Like your own desk at home or work, you can add and remove items from the desktop, rearrange items, or get rid of them by throwing them into the "trash." You can also open items and, much like a drawer in your desk, find other tools or materials you have stored. You can place these items on the desktop, or take items off the desktop and place them in the "drawer." Just like your own desk, your most frequently used items should be on the desktop so you can quickly begin work while those items that you use less frequently should be put away for easy access as needed, just as you might put papers in a drawer or on a nearby shelf.

Note: If your screen is different, it is because your school may have modified the default Windows 95 layout.

The default desktop, shown in Figure 1-3 on the following page, is very simple and contains only a few essential items that are needed to get started using Windows 95. Your desktop may have been customized to include other items.

Read the information in "Parts of the Windows 95 Desktop" on the following page.

Parts of the Windows 95 Desktop

Figure 1-3

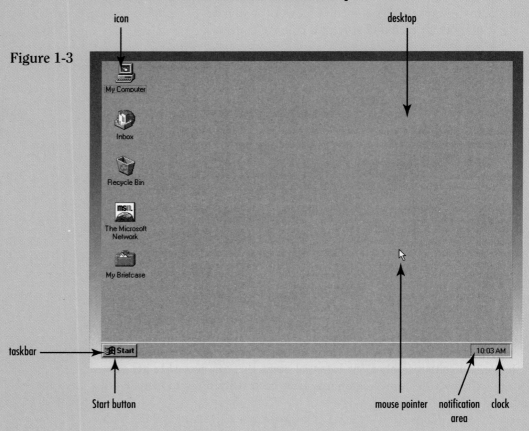

The initial Windows 95 screen displays icons such as My Computer and Recycle Bin. The icon picture generally represents the item.

At the bottom of the screen is the **taskbar.** It displays the **Start button** on the left end of the bar. The Start button is used to start a program, open a document, get help, find files, and change system settings. The center of the taskbar is currently blank. It will display buttons representing currently active tasks as you use Windows, making switching between tasks easy. The clock on the right end of the taskbar displays the time as maintained by your computer. To the left of the clock, is the **notification area**. The notification area will display indicators, such as a printer when printing is in progress or a speaker if your system includes audio hardware.

If your computer is part of a network, the Network Neighborhood icon will appear.

Using the Mouse

The mouse that is attached to your computer displays an arrow-shaped symbol ⬉ on your screen.

Concept 3: The Mouse

The **mouse** is a hand-held hardware device that is attached to your computer. It controls the **mouse pointer** that currently appears on your screen as an arrow. The pointer is controlled by the rubber-coated ball on the bottom of the mouse. This ball must move within its socket for the pointer to move on the screen. The ball moves when the mouse is moved along a flat surface. The ball's movement is translated into signals that tell the computer how to move the onscreen pointer. The direction the ball moves controls the direction the pointer moves on the screen.

Moving the mouse across your desktop moves the pointer in the direction you are moving the mouse. If you pick up the mouse and move it to another location on your work surface, the pointer will not move on the screen. Some computers use a track ball to move the mouse pointer. You move this ball with your fingertips in the direction you want the onscreen pointer to move.

The mouse pointer changes shape on the screen depending on what it is pointing to. Some of the most common shapes are shown in the table below.

Pointer Shape	Meaning
⬉	Select
I	Insert text
⌛	Busy
⊘	Area is not available
⬉?	Displays Help on selected item
↔	Horizontal resize
⬉	Diagonal resize
✛	Move

On top of the mouse are two buttons. These buttons are used to choose items on the screen. The mouse actions and descriptions are shown in the table below.

Action	Description
Point	Move the mouse so the mouse pointer is positioned on the item you want to use
Click	Press and release a mouse button
Double-click	Quickly press and release a mouse button twice
Drag	Move the mouse while holding down a mouse button

OPERATING SYSTEM

Your computer may use a track ball to move the mouse pointer.

This text assumes mouse use. Keyboard tips or alternative ways of doing things will be provided in marginal notes.

Moving the mouse over your work surface moves the mouse pointer on your screen.

Move the mouse in any direction.

The pointer on the screen moved in the direction you moved the mouse.

Move the mouse in all directions (up, down, left, and right) and note the movement and shape of the mouse pointer.

Displaying the Start Menu

As you learn about Windows 95, you will find there are many ways to perform the same task. However, using the Start button is one of the best places to learn how to use Windows 95. It provides quick and easy access to most features you will use frequently.

Move the mouse pointer so that it is on the Start button.

This is called **pointing**. When you hold the mouse pointer over the Start button a box containing the message "Click here to begin" is briefly displayed.

While pointing to the Start button, click the left mouse button.

Your screen should be similar to Figure 1-4.

Figure 1-4

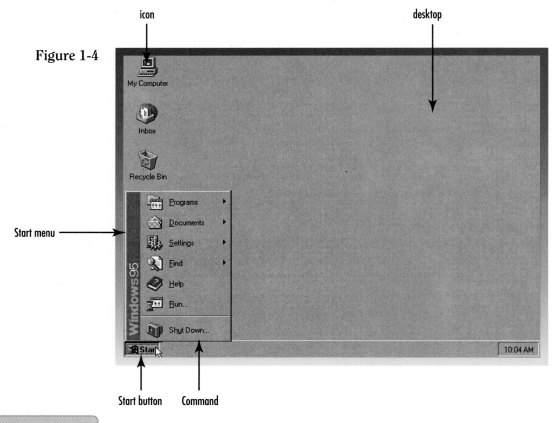

icon   desktop

Start menu

Start button   Command

You can also display the Start menu by pressing Ctrl + Esc.

Clicking on the Start button displays the Start menu. The Start menu is a special Windows 95 menu that is used to access and begin all activities you want to perform on the computer. It is one of many menus you will see in Windows 95.

Concept 4: Menus

A **menu** is one of many methods you can use to tell a program what you want it to do. When opened, a menu displays a list of commands. Most menus can simply be opened by clicking on the menu name, as you did the Start menu.

Many menus appear in a **menu bar** rather than as a button. When chosen, a menu bar command displays a **pull-down menu** of additional commands from which you can select. Other menus pop up when you right-click (click the right mouse button) on an area of the desktop. This type of menu is called a **shortcut menu**. Menus are everywhere in Windows 95, but they all operate in the same way.

Once a menu is open, you can select and choose commands from the menu. **Selecting** a command moves a colored highlight bar, called the **selection cursor**, to the command. Simply pointing to the command moves the selection cursor to it. When a command is selected, this indicates the command will be activated when chosen. You **choose** the selected command by clicking on the command, or by typing the underlined command letter, or by pressing ←Enter. When the command is chosen, the associated action is performed.

Menus may include the following features, (not all menus include all features):

Feature	Meaning
Ellipses (...)	Indicates a dialog box will be displayed
▶	Indicates a cascading menu will be displayed
Dimmed command	Indicates the command is not available for selection until certain other conditions are met
Shortcut key	A key or key combination that can be used to execute a command without using the menu
Checkmark (✔)	Indicates a toggle type of command. Selecting it turns the feature on or off. A checkmark indicates the feature is on
Bullet (•)	Indicates that the commands in that group are mutually exclusive: only one can be selected. The bullet indicates the currently selected feature.

OPERATING SYSTEM

If your system has Microsoft Office 95 installed, your Start menu will include the New Office Document and Open Office Document commands.

Selecting Commands

The basic Start menu consists of a list of seven commands from which you can select. The icons to the left of each command are graphic representations of the command. The commands and what they are used for are described briefly in the table below.

Command	Used to
Programs	Start programs
Documents	Open files and related programs
Settings	Change or view the computer system settings
Find	Locate files
Help	Obtain direct access to the Help feature
Run	Start a program using DOS command-line type functionality
Shut Down	Shut down, restart, and log off the computer

You can also move the selection cursor using the ↑ and ↓ keys.

To select a command, point to Shut Down.

The selection cursor is displayed, indicating the currently selected command.

Point to the Run command and then the Help command.

The selection cursor moves to each command as you point to it. To the right of the Find command, an arrowhead ▶ symbol is displayed, indicating that selecting it will display a submenu of commands. To see the submenu for the Find command,

Point to: Find

Your screen should be similar to Figure 1-5.

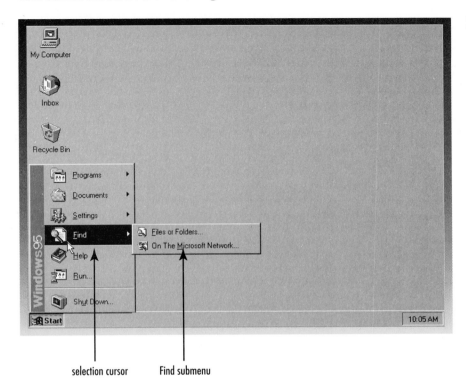

Figure 1-5

selection cursor   Find submenu

The submenu displays two options that can be selected to search for files.

Point to the Settings, Documents, and Programs commands to see the submenu associated with each.

After opening a menu, you may decide you do not want to select a command. To close or cancel the Start menu you can click the Start button again or click anywhere outside the menu box.

Cancel the Start menu.

Developing the skill for moving the mouse and correctly positioning the pointer takes some time. If you accidentally find yourself in the wrong location or in a command that you did not intend to select, cancel the selected menu as you did above and try again.

Choosing Commands

Now that you have learned how to move the mouse pointer and select commands, you are ready to choose a command from the menu. As you learned in Concept 4: Menus, the process of *selecting* a command simply moves the selection cursor to the item, whereas *choosing* performs the action associated with the command. To see how this works, you will choose the Help command from the Start menu. The Help command starts the Help program.

> Pressing ⌐Esc⌐ also cancels menu selections, one menu level at a time.

Concept 5: Help

Windows **Help** is a quick way to find out information about commands or features. It is a separate application that is loaded when you choose the Help command and specify a topic that you want help information on. Help is available in all Windows applications and operates in the same way as Windows Help.

> You can also type the underlined letter of a command to choose it. Command letters to type will appear underlined.

Open the Start menu again.

To choose a command, point to the command and click the left button.

Choose: **Help**

Your screen should be similar to Figure 1-6.

Figure 1-6

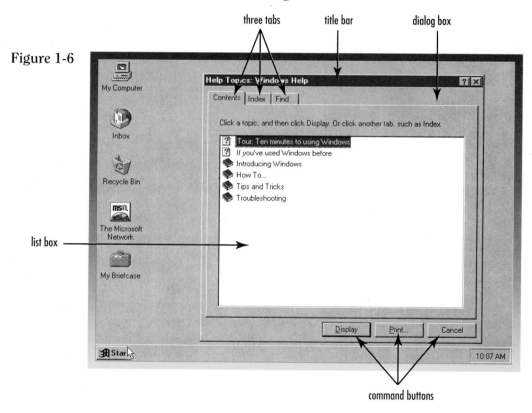

You have executed the Help command, the Start menu is cleared from the screen, and the Help Topics dialog box is displayed.

> Do not be concerned if your Help dialog box displays different information.

Using a Dialog Box

A dialog box is a common feature that is displayed whenever the program requires additional information to complete a command.

Concept 6: Dialog Box

A **dialog box** is how Windows programs provide and request information from you in order to complete a task. All dialog boxes have a **title bar** at the top of the box, which displays a name identifying the contents of the dialog box and buttons. Inside the dialog box are areas to select or specify the needed information, and command buttons. The features shown in the table below may be found in dialog boxes; however, not all features are found in every dialog box.

Feature	Meaning
Close Button ☒	Used to close a dialog box.
What's This ❓	Displays Help on dialog box options.
Text box	An area where you type in the requested information.
Option button ⦿	An option preceded with a circle. The selected option displays a black dot. Only one option can be selected from a list of option buttons.
List box	A box displaying a list of information from which you can select.
Drop-down list box	A text box that displays the currently selected item and a ▾ button. Clicking the ▾ button displays a drop-down list of items from which you can select, or you can type the information in the text box.
Check box ☑	An option preceded with a square. The selected option displays ✔. You can select more than one check box option.
Sliding control	Dragging the lever in the control increases or decreases the related setting, such as volume.
Command button OK	Instructs Windows to carry out the instructions on the button. The two most common command buttons are OK and Cancel. Other buttons you will see are Close, Help, Options, Setup, Display, and Settings.

Many dialog boxes also include folder-like tabs across the top of the dialog box that open to display related options. This type of dialog box is called a **tab dialog box**. The tab names identify the content of the tab. The active tab appears in front of the other tabs and displays the available options for the feature.

The Help topics tab dialog box displays the dialog box name "Help Topics: Windows Help" in the title bar. It also contains three tabs—Contents, Index, and Find—that are used to access the three different means of getting Help information. To select and open a tab, click on it with the mouse. To see the contents of the three tab areas,

You can also press Ctrl + Tab↹ to select the tab to the right or Ctrl + ⇧Shift + Tab↹ to select the tab to the left.

Click: Find

The Find tab is open and displays three numbered areas. Area 1 displays a drop-down list box where you enter a word or phrase you want to locate. Areas 2 and 3 are list boxes. The list boxes display a list of words or topics from which you can select. You will learn shortly how these features work when you use the Index tab.

Click: Contents

The Contents tab (shown in Figure 1-6) is open and displays six items. Double-clicking on an item preceded with a ◈ opens a book and displays additional books or specific Help topics.

Double-click: ◈ **Introducing Windows**

The Introducing Windows book icon appears as an open book and two new book icons appear indented below it.

Double-click: ◈ **Welcome**

Three items appear under the Welcome book.

Topics preceded with a ? display a Help window of information on that topic when chosen. You will open a Help window from the Index tab next. The Index tab is the area you will probably use the most often.

Click: Index

Your screen should be similar to Figure 1-7.

"Double-click" means to click the left mouse button twice in rapid succession without moving the mouse.

Figure 1-7

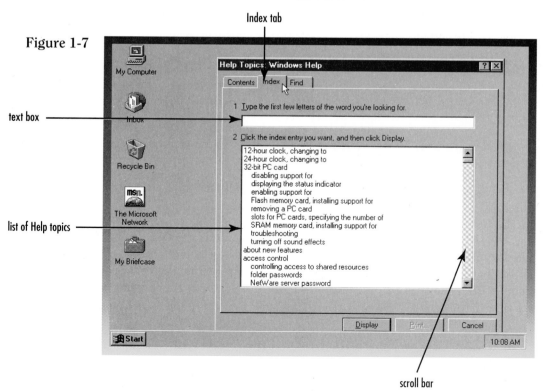

Index tab

text box

list of Help topics

scroll bar

The Index tab has two numbered areas. Area 1 consists of a text box where you can type a word or phrase that best describes the topic you want to locate. Area 2 is a list box displaying a complete list of Help topics in alphabetical order.

Using Scroll Bars

The topic list box contains many more topics than can be displayed at one time in the box. Whenever there is more information than can be displayed in a window or list box, a scroll bar is displayed.

Concept 7: Scroll Bar

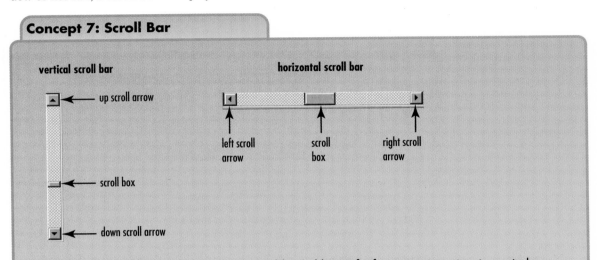

A **scroll bar** is used with a mouse to bring additional lines of information into view in a window or list box. Scroll bars can run vertically along the right side or horizontally along the bottom of a window or list box. The vertical scroll bar is used to move vertically and the horizontal scroll bar moves horizontally in the space. The scroll bar consists of **scroll arrows** and a **scroll box**. Clicking the arrows moves the information in the direction of the arrows, allowing new topics to be displayed in the space.

You can also move to a general location within the area by dragging the scroll box up or down the scroll bar. The location of the scroll box on the scroll bar indicates your relative position within the area of available information. In many scroll bars, the size of the scroll box also indicates the relative amount of the information that is available. For example, a small box indicates that only a small amount of the total available information is displayed, whereas a large box indicates that almost all or a large portion of the total amount of available information is displayed.

To bring more topics into view, you will scroll the list using the scroll bar.

Point to the down scroll arrow in the list box and click the left mouse button five times.

The list of topics has moved up line by line, allowing new topics to be displayed at the bottom of the box.

To continuously scroll the list, point to the down scroll arrow and hold down the left mouse button for a few seconds.

The list has moved down continuously, line by line.

Point to the up scroll arrow and click several times.

Press [Tab ⇆] to move from one area in a dialog box to another, and use the [↓] or [↑] directional keys to scroll a list line by line.

OPERATING SYSTEM

The list scrolled up several lines. Did you notice the movement of the scroll box as you scrolled the list? It moves up or down along the scroll bar to show your relative location within the list.

Click on the scroll bar below the scroll box several times.

Clicking above or below the scroll box moves the list up or down a boxful of topics at a time.

Click above the scroll box.

Dragging the scroll box moves to a general location within the list.

Drag the scroll box to the lower third of the scroll bar.

Your screen should be similar to Figure 1-8.

Press [Page Up] and [Page Down] to move a boxful at a time.

Figure 1-8

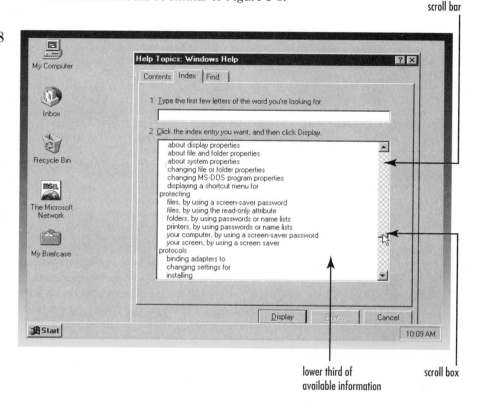

scroll bar

lower third of available information

scroll box

The location of the scroll box in the lower third of the bar indicates the information you see in the list is in the lower third of available information.

Drag the scroll box to the top of the scroll bar.

The features you have learned to scroll a list in this dialog box can be used to scroll whenever a scroll bar appears.

When the topic you want help on appears, click on it to select it.

Click on any topic in the list.

The selection cursor highlights the selected topic and the topic appears in the text box.

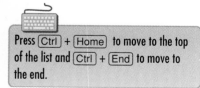

Press [Ctrl] + [Home] to move to the top of the list and [Ctrl] + [End] to move to the end.

Getting Help on a Topic

An easier way to locate a topic is to type the first few letters of the topic in the text box. To see how this works, you will locate Help on formatting a disk.

To quickly move to the formatting topic in the list box, you will type the word "format" in the text box. The text box must be active before you can type information in it. When active, a blinking vertical bar called the **insertion point** is displayed or the information in the text box is highlighted. To activate the text box,

Click on: the text box

The insertion point appears in the text box. Because the box displays a topic, the insertion point is positioned in the topic text wherever you were pointing when you clicked the mouse. The mouse pointer appears as an I-beam in the text box. It is used to position the insertion point.

Before you can type the new text, you need to clear the current entry. To do this, you could use ⟮←Backspace⟯ or ⟮Del⟯ to remove each character one character at a time. Another way is to select or highlight the entry and then type the new entry. To select text displayed in a text box, you drag the mouse pointer from one end of the entry to the other.

Select the text in the text box.

The entire entry should appear highlighted, indicating that it is selected.

Now, as soon as you begin typing, the existing entry will be cleared and replaced by the text you are typing.

Type: f

Refer to Concept 6: Dialog Box for information on text boxes.

Press ⟮Tab⟯ or ⟮Ctrl⟯ + ⟮Tab⟯ to move to and activate different areas of the dialog box. Buttons and list boxes display a dotted box when active, and text boxes highlight existing entries and display the insertion point.

"Drag" means to hold down the left mouse button while moving the mouse.

Your screen should be similar to Figure 1-9.

Figure 1-9

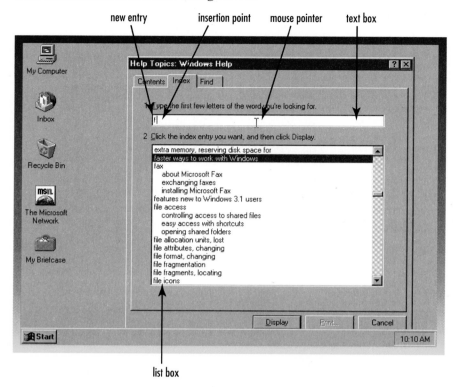

new entry   insertion point   mouse pointer   text box

list box

The selection cursor jumps to the first word in the topic list beginning with the letter "f." If you scrolled this list, you would eventually locate the word "format." To narrow the list even more, you will type the next letter of the word.

Type: o

The selection cursor now jumps to the first topic beginning with "fo." To continue to narrow the list,

Type: r

> If you make a typing error, use ⟨←Backspace⟩ to erase characters to the left of the insertion point and retype the entry correctly.

The selection cursor now highlights the first word beginning with "for" and the formatting topic is now visible in the list. The "disks" subhead under the formatting topic is the topic you want help on.

Select: disks

Your screen should be similar to Figure 1-10.

selected topic displayed
in text box

selected topic highlighted
with selection cursor

Figure 1-10

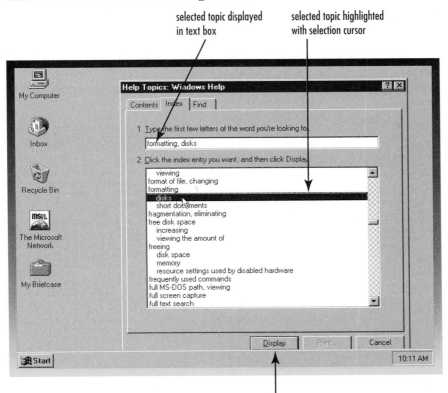

shows Help window on selected topic

The selection cursor should be highlighting the word "disks" and the complete topic, "formatting, disks," appears in the text box.

The bottom of the dialog box displays three command buttons. As the name in the button indicates, Display is used to display the selected topic, Print is used to print the selected topic, and Cancel is used to close the Help dialog box. To display the Help information on the selected topic,

Choose: Display

Command buttons that appear dimmed are not currently available for selection.

You can also double-click on the topic in the list box to both select it and to choose Display.

To choose command buttons, type the underlined letter or select the button and press ⏎Enter.

Your screen should be similar to Figure 1-11.

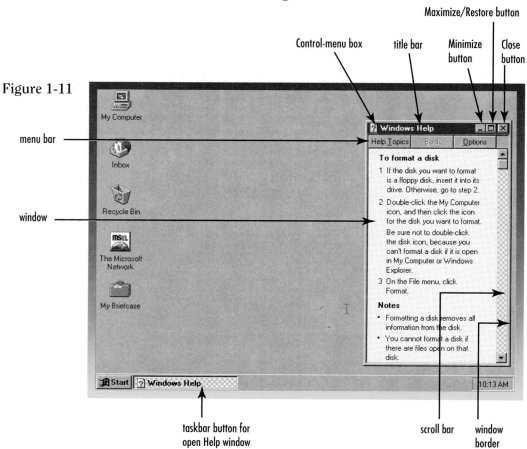

Figure 1-11

A Help window of information on how to format a disk is displayed. The title bar displays the application name, Windows Help. The menu bar displays three menu buttons that are used to access Help features.

Concept 8: Window

As you learned in Concept 1: What's Windows 95?, a window is a rectangular section of the screen that is dedicated to a specific activity or application. The **window border** outlines the window. All windows have the basic parts described below:

Feature	Meaning
Title bar	A bar located at the top of the window that displays the application name and buttons.
Control-menu box	An icon located on the left end of the title bar that when opened, displays the Control menu. This consists of a list of commands that are used to move, size, and otherwise control the window.
Minimize button 🔲	Used to reduce a window to a its smallest size.
Maximize/Restore button 🔲/🔲	Used to enlarge a window to its maximum size. Changes to 🔲 when maximized to allow you to return the window to its previous size.
Close button ☒	Used to exit the application running in the window and to close the window.
Menu bar	A bar located below the title bar, containing a list of menus that can be used with the application displayed in the window.

A scroll bar also appears in many windows whenever the window cannot fully display the information. Some windows also have additional features such as a toolbar and status bar, which will be described later in these labs.

All applications that you open are displayed in their own window. In addition, the taskbar displays a button for each open window. The button appears depressed, indicating the window is the **active window** or the window that is currently in use. Multiple windows can be open on the desktop at once, but only one window is active at a time.

Do not confuse a window and a dialog box. A window always includes a menu bar and does not display command buttons.

Moving Windows

Sometimes, when a window is displayed, it overlaps other information on the desktop. To see the area under the window, you can easily move it.

Concept 9: Moving Windows

When a window opens, it can appear anywhere on your desktop. Sometimes the location of the window is inconvenient. Moving a window simply displays the window at another location on the desktop. It does not change the size of the window.

A window is moved by pointing to the title bar and dragging an outline of the window to the new location on the desktop.

A dialog box can be moved just like a window.

Open the Control menu (press [Alt] + [Spacebar]) and select Move. Then use the directional keys to specify the direction to move. Press [←Enter] when done.

With the pointer anywhere within the Help title bar, click and drag the mouse. Do not release the mouse button.

An outline of the window is displayed as you drag it across the desktop. When you release the button, the window moves to the new location.

Move the Help window to the center of the desktop and release the mouse button.

Your screen should be similar to Figure 1-12.

Figure 1-12

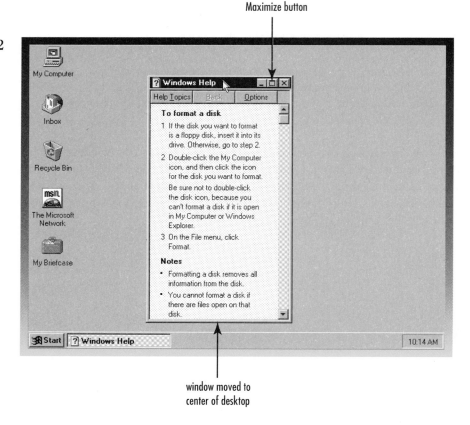

Maximize button

window moved to
center of desktop

Sizing Windows

Windows appear on the desktop in different sizes, and sometimes the current size is too small or too large. The size of a window can easily be changed.

Concept 10: Sizing Windows

The size of a window can be changed to just about any size you want. A window can be **minimized** to its smallest size using the ▬ Minimize button, or **maximized** to its largest size using the ▢ Maximize button. A maximized window can then be **restored** to its previous size using the ▣ Restore button. In addition, a window can be custom sized by pointing to the window border and dragging the border in the direction you want to go. Dragging inward decreases the size and dragging outward increases the size. Dragging a corner increases or decreases the size, of the two adjoining borders at the same time.

A dialog box cannot be sized.

Notice that a scroll bar appears along the edge of the window. This indicates there is more information that cannot be displayed in the window space. To enlarge the window to its maximum size,

Click: ▢ Maximize

Open the Control menu (⟨Alt⟩ + ⟨Spacebar⟩) and select Maximize.

The Help window now occupies the entire desktop. Because all the information can be displayed in the window, the scroll bar is not displayed.

Read the information about formatting a disk.

Notice that the Maximize button has changed to ▣. This is the Restore button. Restoring a window returns it to its previous size and location.

Click: ▣ Restore

Select Restore from the Control menu.

You can also custom size and shape a window by adjusting the window borders. When you point to a border or corner, the mouse pointer changes to a two-headed arrow ↔. The directions in which the arrowheads point indicate the directions you can drag the border or corner.

Point to the lower right corner of the Help window. (The pointer is correctly positioned when the pointer changes to a two-headed diagonal arrow ↘.)

As you drag the mouse, an outline of the window will appear showing you the new size.

Reduce the window size to about a 2-inch square and then release the button.

Select Size from the Control menu and then use the directional keys to position the ✥ and to specify the direction to size. Press ⟨←Enter⟩ when done.

OPERATING SYSTEM

Your screen should be similar to Figure 1-13.

Figure 1-13

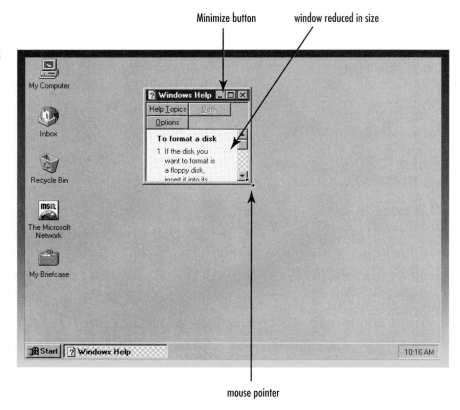

Minimize button   window reduced in size

mouse pointer

As much of the Help information as possible is displayed in the window. To view the rest of the information, you would need to scroll the window.

Once a window has been custom sized, the only way to return it to the original size is by dragging the borders again.

Enlarge the Help window to its original size (see Figure 1-12).

Often you will want to keep a window open for future reference, but you do not want it to occupy space on the desktop. To do this, you can minimize the window.

Select Minimize from the Control menu.

Click: ▬ **Minimize**

Your screen should be similar to Figure 1-14.

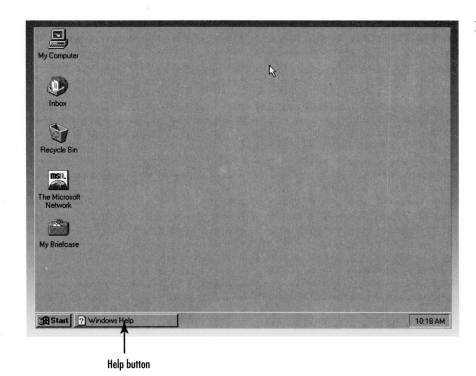

Figure 1-14

Help button

The Help window is minimized. Notice that the Windows Help button in the taskbar is still displayed. This indicates the window is still open, but minimized. To redisplay the Help window, simply click on its taskbar button.

Click:

The window is redisplayed on the screen. Now, you can either close the Help window or return to the Help topics dialog box. Returning to the dialog box is often useful if the topic you selected does not provide the information you need. To return,

Choose: **Help Topics**

The last topic selected is still highlighted. Now you could use the Help dialog box to display information on other Help topics in the Help window. However, the information the Help window currently displays is appropriate. To close the dialog box,

Choose: Cancel
or
Click: ☒

The ☒ button is located at the right end of the title bar.

OPERATING SYSTEM

The dialog box is closed, but the Help window that was under the dialog box is still open and is now visible.

Note: If you are running short on lab time, you can quite before beginning Part 2. To do this, close the Help window, then follow the directions to quit Windows 95 on page WN49. When you begin Part 2, display the Help window on formatting a disk.

Part 2

Formatting a Disk

You would like to keep the Help on how to format a disk open so you can refer to the directions while you are formatting a disk next.

To see more of the desktop, move the Help window back to the right edge of the desktop (as in Figure 1-11).

You will format a new disk so you can copy the data files needed to complete the next two labs to the new disk.

Concept 11: Formatting a Disk

Before a new disk can be used, you must **format** or convert it from a generic state into a format that can be used by your computer. Many disks are shipped from the manufacturer in a blank (**unformatted**) form so they can be used by a variety of computers. Others are preformatted and do not need to be formatted before use.

Formatting prepares a new disk to accept information and files. Specifically, it sets up and labels the **tracks** (concentric rings where data is stored on the disk) and **sectors** (divisions of the tracks) to accept information. It checks the tracks for any bad spots that are unable to store information and marks off these areas so they cannot be used. It also sets up the area on the disk where the directory of files will be maintained.

Any disk, old or new, can be formatted. However, if you format a used disk, any files or information on it will be erased during formatting. Be careful only to format disks that do not contain information that you may want. Be especially careful when formatting that you do not accidentally format the hard disk, as all your programs and files will be erased. If you attempt to format the hard disk, Windows displays a warning message.

Even if your disk is preformatted, you can complete the directions below and format it again.

Following the directions in Step 1 of the Help window, place a blank floppy disk in the appropriate drive.

Next, following the directions in Step 2,

A single click on an icon selects (highlights) it, and a double-click opens it.

Double-click:
My Computer

Your screen should be similar to Figure 1-15.

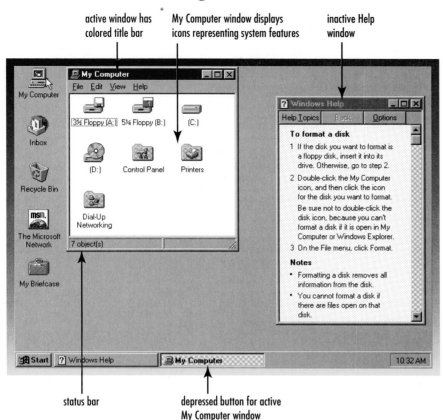

active window has
colored title bar

My Computer window displays
icons representing system features

inactive Help
window

Figure 1-15

status bar

depressed button for active
My Computer window

A second window is open on the desktop, and the taskbar displays a new button for this open window. The My Computer window is the active window. You can tell it is the active window because the taskbar button is depressed and the window title bar is colored. The My Computer window is used to view the information on your computer. It displays icons representing various features associated with your computer. Some or all of the items shown in the table below may be displayed in your My Computer window.

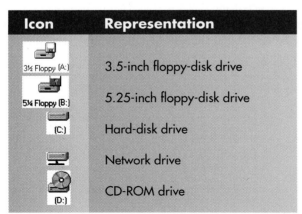

Icon	Representation
3½ Floppy (A:)	3.5-inch floppy-disk drive
5¼ Floppy (B:)	5.25-inch floppy-disk drive
(C:)	Hard-disk drive
	Network drive
(D:)	CD-ROM drive

If the status bar is not displayed, after formatting your disk, you can turn it on by choosing Status Bar from the View menu.

In addition, at the bottom of the window a status bar is displayed.

Concept 12: Status Bar

Many windows display a **status bar** at the bottom of the window. The information displayed in the status bar varies with the program you are using and the task being performed. The purpose of the status bar is to advise you of the status of different program conditions and features as you use the program.

Currently the status bar tells you the number of items, called objects, in the window.

Still following the directions in Step 2, to select the drive that contains the disk to be formatted.

Do not double-click the disk icon, because this opens the disk and you cannot format a disk if it is open in My Computer.

Click: 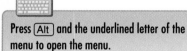 (or the appropriate drive for your station)

The drive icon is highlighted, indicating it is selected. Also notice that the status bar indicates that one object is selected.

Finally, to begin formatting the disk, following the instructions in Step 3, you use the Format command on the File menu. To open the File menu,

Press [Alt] and the underlined letter of the menu to open the menu.

Click: File

Refer to Concept 4: Menus to review menu features.

A pull-down menu of File commands is displayed. Pull-down menus operate just like the Start menu. They include the same features as the Start menu, except they do not display icons. Horizontal lines within many menus divide the commands into related groups. Also notice that the status bar displays a brief description of what the selected File menu command does.

If the status bar is covered by the pull-down menu, make the My Computer window larger.

To select the Format command,

Point to: Format

The Format command is selected and now the status bar displays a description for the selected command. Notice that the Format command displays ellipses. This indicates that a dialog box will appear when the command is chosen. To choose the Format command,

Click: Format

Your screen should be similar to Figure 1-16.

Format dialog box   What's this?
button

Figure 1-16

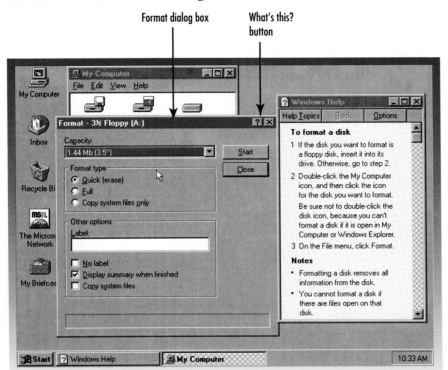

The Format dialog box is displayed. Another feature frequently found in dialog boxes is the 🔲 "What's this" button located at the right end of the title bar. It is used to get Help on the dialog box options. To do this,

Click: 🔲 What's this?

The mouse pointer changes to a ⌖?, indicating it will provide brief Help information about any item in the dialog box that you click on. The first dialog box option is used to specify the capacity of the disk. **Capacity** refers to the maximum number of bytes the disk can hold. To get help on this option,

Click: Capacity

If necessary, move the dialog box to see the 🔲 button.

Not all dialog boxes have a 🔲 button. To get Help on using these boxes, use the Help command button if available or try pressing F1 .

Your screen should be similar to Figure 1-17.

Figure 1-17

definition of "capacity" in pop-up window

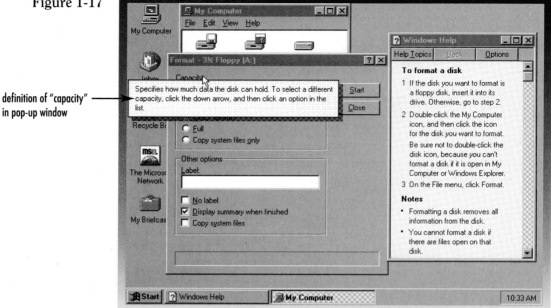

A pop-up window containing an explanation of what the Capacity option does is displayed.

Read the information provided in the window. Then, to close the pop-up window, click inside the box.

Windows assumes that you want to format the disk with the maximum capacity for the drive. Not all types of floppy disks are compatible with all types of floppy-disk drives. Generally, a disk can be formatted at a capacity less than or equal to the capacity of the disk drive. For example, to format a disk at 720K in a disk drive that has a maximum capacity of 1.44MB, you would change the capacity to 720K in the capacity list box. If you are unsure of the size of the drive or disk, check with your instructor.

If necessary, change the capacity to the size of the disk you are formatting.

The Format Type section of the dialog box displays three options: Quick (erase), Full, and Copy System Files Only. Quick format is used only on previously formatted disks that you know are in good condition. It does not check for bad spots on the disk. Full performs a complete format and is always used on new disks. The Copy System Files Only option will copy system files to a formatted disk without removing any existing files.

Use ☑ What's this? to get more information about the format types.

You can also press (Esc) to close the pop-up window.

To display the drop-down list of Capacity options, click ☑ or press (↓).

The Format Type options are preceded with option buttons, indicating only one can be selected. The best format option for your purpose is Full. To select Full,

Click: Full

Press [Tab ↹] to move to different areas of the dialog box.

The last area in the dialog box contains several additional check box options. Any number of these options can be selected.

Use ☑ What's this? to read information on each option.

You want to include a label on the disk that will display your name. This is an electronic label that is recorded during the formatting process. If the No Label check box is selected (that is, if it displays a ✔), you will need to clear the selection first.

If necessary, clear the checkmark from the No label option.

Then, to specify the label to include on your disk, click in the Label text box.

Type: **your first initial and as much of your last name as possible**

The disk label can contain up to 11 characters including spaces.

You want Windows to display the summary information when formatting is done and you do not want the system files copied to your disk.

If necessary, select the Display Summary When Finished option and deselect the Copy System Files option.

Your screen should be similar to Figure 1-18.

selected option button   Start button begins formatting

Figure 1-18

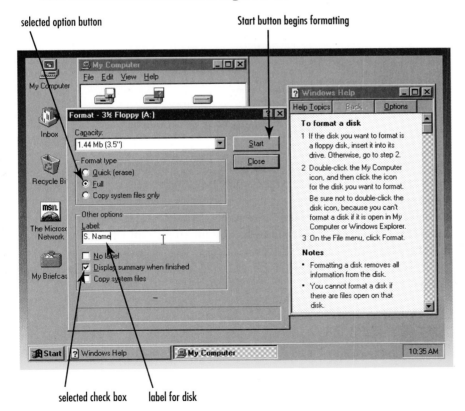

selected check box   label for disk

To carry out the command to format the disk in the drive specified using the settings you have selected in the dialog box,

> If an informational dialog box appears indicating there is no disk in the drive, follow the directions in the box and choose Retry.

Click: Start

Notice the Formatting progress bar at the bottom of the dialog box. It indicates how much of the formatting task is completed. When formatting is complete, your screen should be similar to Figure 1-19.

Figure 1-19

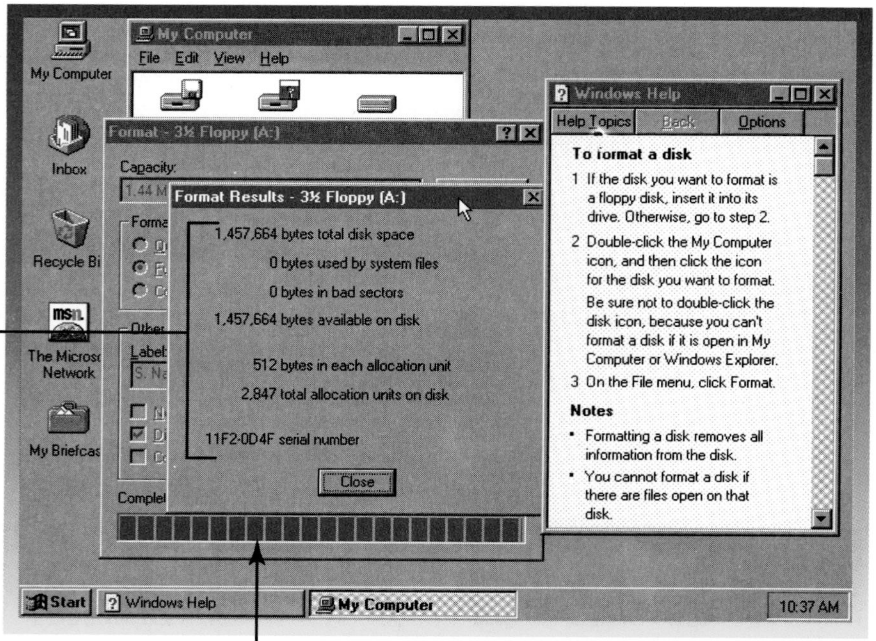

formatting results

Formatting progress bar

The Format Results dialog box is displayed. It shows the total number of bytes on the disk and bytes available for use. If any bad sectors were located, Windows tells you the number of bytes in bad sectors. The number of bytes available in each allocation unit, how many allocation units were created (indicates how Windows has divided the disk for file storage into groups or sectors), and the serial number are also displayed.

You have formatted your disk, and it is now ready to be used. To close the Format Results dialog box,

Choose: Close

> You could also click ☒ to close the dialog box.

The Format dialog box is still open, allowing you to format another disk. To close the Format dialog box,

> If you need to format additional disks, repeat the procedure.

Choose: Close

The My Computer window is active again.

Now that you know how to use menus, if necessary, turn on the display of the status bar (<u>V</u>iew/Status <u>B</u>ar).

Viewing Disk Properties

Next, you would like to see the properties associated with the newly formatted disk.

> ### Concept 13: Properties
>
> **Properties** are the settings and attributes associated with an object on the screen such as an icon. Just about all the objects on the desktop have properties associated with them. The desktop itself is an object that has properties. The properties can be viewed and changed if necessary to suit your needs.

To view the properties associated with the disk in your floppy drive,

Right-click: 3½ Floppy (A:)   **(or other appropriate drive)**

Your screen should be similar to Figure 1-20.

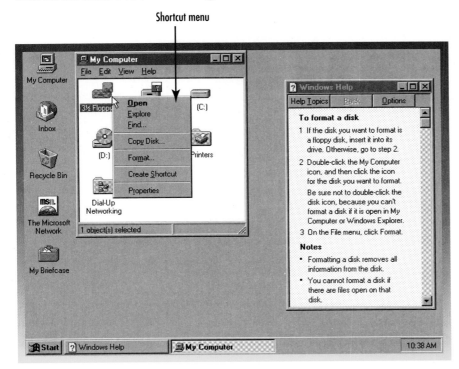

Figure 1-20

A shortcut menu of options appears. Shortcut menus appear whenever you right-click an item on the desktop. The options in the shortcut menu vary with the item that is clicked on.

> The Properties command can also be selected from the File menu.

Choose: Properties

The Properties tab dialog box is displayed. It includes two tabs that access different options associated with Disk properties.

If necessary, select the General tab.

Your screen should be similar to Figure 1-21.

disk label   type of disk

Figure 1-21

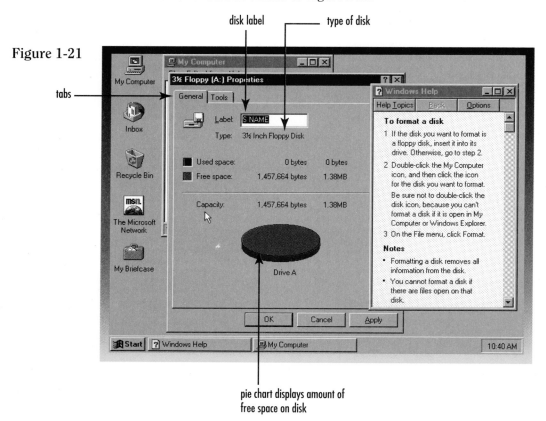

tabs

pie chart displays amount of
free space on disk

The Label text box displays the disk label you entered during formatting. If needed, you can change the label on a disk using this text box. Below the Label text box, the type of disk is identified.

The General tab also displays information on the amount of used and free space on the disk. Since this disk is newly formatted, it does not contain any data. The capacity value indicates the total capacity available on the disk. This value should equal the amount of free and used space. Finally, a pie chart visually displays the amount of free and used space. Again, because this disk is newly formatted, the chart shows that the disk is 100 percent unused.

Close the Properties dialog box.

Remove the newly formatted disk from the drive. To show that this disk has been formatted, put a paper label on it. Include your name and other identifying information such as the class, and the words "Windows 95 DATA DISK" on the label.

Now that your disk has been formatted, it is ready to be used to store information. You will use this disk to hold a copy of the files you will need to complete the next two Windows 95 labs. You will learn how to copy files to the disk in Lab 2.

With formatting finished, you can close the My Computer and Help windows. To close the My Computer window,

Click:

The My Computer button is also removed from the taskbar.

In a similar manner, close the Help window.

> Choose Cancel or click .

> If you are using 5.25-inch disks and you need to write on a label that is already on a disk, use a felt-tip pen only.

> You could also choose Close from the File menu to close a window.

> Choose Close from the Control menu or press `Alt` + `F4` to close the Help window.

Quitting Windows 95

To avoid damaging files, always follow the procedure below to shut down Windows 95 before you turn off your computer.

When you want to stop working with Windows 95 and turn off your computer, always use the Shut Down command in the Start menu.

Click: **Start**
Choose: **Sh*u*t Down**

The Shut Down Windows dialog box is displayed. It contains options for turning off your computer. These options have the following effects:

> Your Shut Down dialog box may not include all options listed.

Option	Effect
Shut down the computer?	Saves any settings you have changed in Windows 95 and prepares the computer to be turned off
Restart the computer?	Saves any settings you have changed in Windows 95 and restarts computer
Restart the computer in MS-DOS mode?	Saves any settings you have changed in Windows 95 and restarts computer in MS-DOS mode. This mode is needed to run DOS programs that will not run under Windows 95.
Close all programs and log-on as a different user?	If your computer is connected to a network, this option is displayed. It disconnects you from a network and prepares the computer to be used by someone else.

> Choosing No cancels the Shut Down Windows dialog box and returns you to your Windows 95 session.

Select the option as directed by your instructor.

Choose: <u>Y</u>es

If you choose Shut Down the Computer, *do not* turn off your computer until you see the message indicating it is safe to do so.

LAB REVIEW

■ ■ ■ ■ ■ ■ ■ ■ ■ ■

Key Terms

active window   WN35
capacity   WN43
choose   WN23
cold start   WN16
common user interface   WN16
desktop   WN19
dialog box   WN27
format   WN40
graphical user interface   WN16
Help   WN26
icon   WN16
insertion point   WN31
maximize   WN37
menu   WN23
menu bar   WN23
minimize   WN37
mouse   WN21
mouse pointer   WN21
notification area   WN20
operating system   WN15
pointing   WN22

properties   WN47
pull-down menu   WN23
restore   WN37
scroll arrow   WN29
scroll bar   WN29
scroll box   WN29
sectors   WN40
select   WN23
selection cursor   WN23
shortcut menu   WN23
Start button   WN20
status bar   WN42
tab dialog box   WN27
taskbar   WN20
title bar   WN27
track   WN40
unformatted   WN40
warm start   WN16
window   WN16
window border   WN35

Command Summary

Command	Action
Start Menu	
Help	Opens Windows Help program
Sh**u**t Down	@Afely shuts downs your computer before you turn the power off
My Computer	
File/For**m**at	Sets up a disk for use
View/Status **B**ar	Turns on/off display of status bar

Matching

1. Match the following with the correct definition or function.

1. (C:)   _____ **a.** button that restores a maximized
                                                window

2. scroll bar   _____ **b.** a mouse pointer

3. window border   _____ **c.** where you point to change the size
                                                of a window

4. formatting   _____ **d.** used to provide information to
                                                complete a command

5. dialog box   _____ **e.** icon for a hard-disk drive

6. ▷   _____ **f.** settings associated with an object

7. properties   _____ **g.** used to bring additional information
                                                into a window

8. ▣   _____ **h.** rectangular section dedicated to a
                                                specific activity or application

9. window   _____ **i.** prepares a disk for use

10. ☒   _____ **j.** closes a window

2. Use the figure below to match each action with its result.

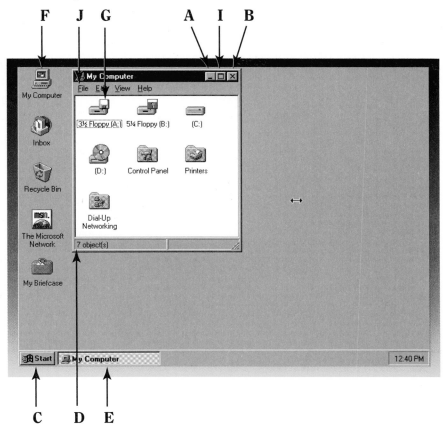

Action

1. click E

2. right-click G

3. click I

4. click G

5. click C

6. click B

7. double-click F

8. click I

9. drag D

10. click A

Result

_____ **a.** displays properties of disk in A drive

_____ **b.** selects the A drive icon

_____ **c.** sizes the window

_____ **d.** minimizes the window

_____ **e.** maximizes the window

_____ **f.** closes the window

_____ **g.** opens the Start menu

_____ **h.** displays File drop-down menu

_____ **i.** restores a minimized window

_____ **j.** opens the My Computer window

3. In the following Windows 95 screen, several items are identified by letters. Enter the correct term for each item in the space provided.

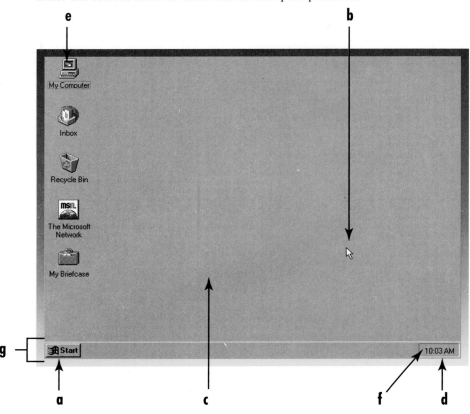

a. _____

b. _____

c. _____

d. _____

e. _____

f. _____

g. _____

4. In the following window, several items are identified by letters. Enter the correct term for each item in the space provided.

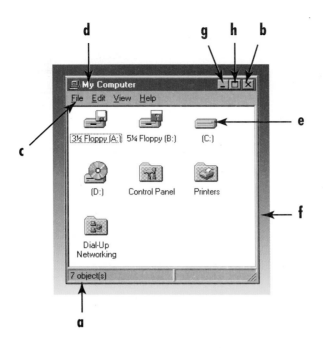

a. _____

b. _____

c. _____

d. _____

e. _____

f. _____

g. _____

h. _____

5. Identify the parts of a dialog box by entering the correct term for each item in the space provided.

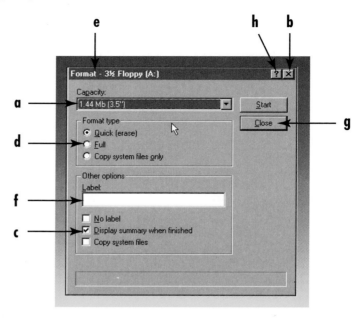

a. _____

b. _____

c. _____

d. _____

e. _____

f. _____

g. _____

h. _____

6. Answer the following with respect to the floppy-disk properties shown below.

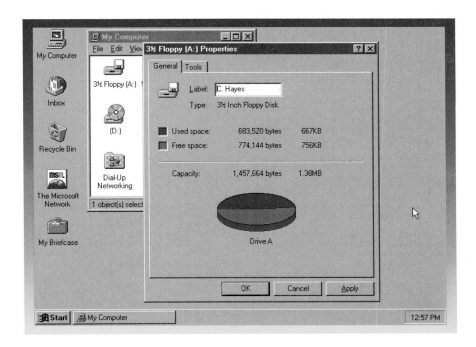

    a. What is the total used disk space? _____

    b. What is the total unused disk space? _____

    c. What is the total number of available bytes? _____

    d. What is the disk label? _____

    e. What is the type of disk? _____

Fill-In Questions

1. Complete the following statements by filling in the blanks with the correct terms.

    a. The _____ program controls computer system resources and coordinates the flow of data to input and output devices.

    b. If your computer is not on, turning on the computer and starting Windows 95 is called a _____.

    c. The _____ button is used to start a program, open a document, get help, find files, and change system settings.

    d. Quickly pressing and releasing the mouse button twice is called _____.

    e. The _____ is a colored highlight that indicates the currently selected command.

f. The _____ is used with a mouse to bring additional lines of information into view.

g. When the taskbar button appears depressed this indicates the window is the _____ window.

h. Before a new disk can be used, it must be _____ from its generic state into a form that can be used by your computer.

i. _____ are settings and attributes associated with an object.

j. To avoid damaging files, always use the _____ commands before you turn off your computer.

HANDS-ON PRACTICE EXERCISES

Step by Step   **Rating System**   ☆ Easy
                                                             ☆☆ Moderate
                                                           ☆☆☆ Difficult

☆

> You need the Windows 95 CD, or the Tour must be loaded on your system before you can complete this problem. Your instructor will provide you with instructions for loading the Tour of Windows 95.

1. The Windows 95 program includes a Tour of Windows 95 that introduces and explains many of the basic Windows features. This problem will use the Tour of Windows 95 to reinforce many of the features presented in this lab.

a. Load the Tour of Windows 95.

b. Choose Using Help from the Welcome to Windows 95 Tour menu.

c. As you read and work through the Using Help tour, answer the following questions:

   1) What feature do you get help on? _____

   2) How did you display the Help topic?_____

   3) What type of button did you use to see the properties dialog box?_____

   4) How did you display a definition in the dialog box?_____

d. Exit the Tour by clicking Exit and the Exit Tour.

☆

2. In this problem you will expand your knowledge of Windows 95 by using Help to find out about and open the Calculator accessory.

a. Open Help and use the Index tab to learn how to start the Calculator.

b. Use the shortcut button in the Help window to start the Calculator application.

c. Use the Calculator Help menu to open Calculator Help and to learn more about the Calculator application. Briefly explain the Calculator accessory features.

d. Using Help as a guide, use the Calculator in standard and scientific views to perform the following calculations; write the answers in the spaces provided.

    1. $6 + 18 + 34 =$ _____

    2. $8432 \times 4324328 =$ _____

    3. $939 \div 83 =$ _____

    4. Average of 34, 84, 283, 231, 423 = _____

    5. Square root of 343 = _____

e. Close Calculator Help. Close the Calculator window.

3. In the lab you learned to use the Index tab of Help. In this problem, you will use the Help Contents and Find tabs to learn more about using Help, to print Help topics, and to locate information about changing the mouse properties.

a. Start Help and display the Contents tab. The Tips and Tricks book contains many hints about how to best use Windows 95.

b. Open the Tips and Tricks book and then the Tips of the Day book.

c. Read the Help information on Using Help.

d. The Options menu in the Help menu bar contains a Print Topic command that will print a copy of the contents of the displayed Help window. Use this command to print the Using Help window of information.

> Before printing, make sure your printer is on and is ready to print.

Next, you will use the Help Find tab to locate information about mouse properties.

e. Return to the Help Topics dialog box and display the Find tab. The Find tab operates much like the Index tab.

f. Enter a word or words in the text box to search for information on changing the speed of your mouse pointer. Then display the Help window on this topic.

g. This Help window includes a shortcut button ▣. Click on this button to open the mouse properties dialog box. Look through all the tabs in the dialog box and use the ▣ Help button in the dialog box to find out about areas or settings you may not understand. What are some of the mouse property settings and why would you want to change these settings? Cancel the dialog box when you are done.

   h. In the motion tab, adjust the pointer speed and turn on the show pointer trails options. Move the mouse to see the results of your selections.

   i. Close the Help window.

4. The character or font size of information in the Help windows can be changed by making it larger so it is easier to read, or smaller so more information is displayed in the window.

   a. Use the Help Index tab to learn how to change the font size of a Help topic.

   b. Try out the different size options.

   c. Print the Help topic with the font size of small.

   d. Return the font size to normal.

   e. Close all open windows.

5. As you learned in the lab, windows can be both sized and moved. This is an important skill to develop because many times windows will cover other information you want to see or may be an inappropriate size when they are opened. To develop this skill you will open, move, and size several windows.

   a. Open the My Computer window.

   b. Display a Help window on changing the clock.

   c. Move the Help window to the lower right corner of the screen.

   d. Move the My Computer window to the upper left corner of the screen.

   e. Size the My Computer window until it covers the left half of the desktop.

   f. Size the Help window until it covers the right half of the desktop.

   g. Return the windows to their approximate original size.

   h. Minimize the My Computer window. Redisplay the window, maximize it, then restore it.

   i. Close all open windows.

On Your Own

6. Every item on the desktop has properties associated with it that can be changed to suit your needs. Display the properties associated with the desktop. Try changing several of the property settings and preview how they would look in the sample area of the tab. Write down the settings that you changed and the effect the changes would have on the desktop. Cancel the dialog box.

7. In the lab you displayed the properties associated with the floppy disk. Display the properties associated with the hard disk and answer the following questions:

- How much free space is on the disk?

- How much space is used on the disk?

- How many megabytes can the drive hold?

8. Read several articles about Windows 95. Identify and describe five new features of the program, for example, Plug-and-play and 32-bit architecture.

9. If you were the operations manager of a large company and had to decide whether to upgrade to Windows 95, what factors would you need to take into consideration? For example, what are the minimum hardware requirements to use Windows 95 effectively, and will the current hardware at your company need to be upgraded? At what cost? With what benefits?

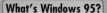
Windows 95: Basic Skills

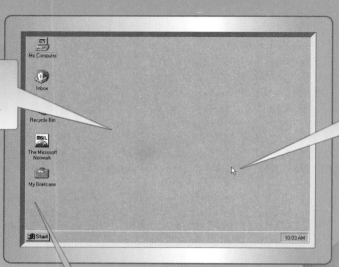

What's Windows 95?

Windows 95 is a graphical operating system program that controls all parts of a computer.

The Mouse

The mouse is a hand-held hardware device that controls an arrow, called a pointer, on the screen.

The Desktop

The Windows 95 screen, called the desktop, displays icons that represent various tools and features.

Concepts

What's Windows 95?
The Desktop
The Mouse

Help
Dialog Box
Scroll Bar

Window
Moving Windows
Sizing Windows

Formatting

Menus
Status Bar
Properties

Window

A window is a rectangular section of the screen that is dedicated to a specific activity or application.

Sizing Windows

Sizing a window makes it larger or smaller, allowing more or less information to appear in the window.

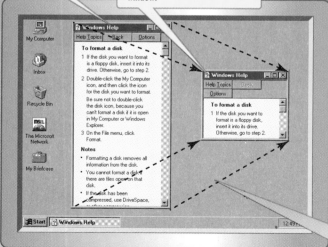

Moving Windows

Moving a window displays the window at another location on the desktop.

Help

The Help facility displays on-screen information about a program's features.

Dialog Box

A dialog box is used to enter information needed to complete a task.

Scroll Bar

A scroll bar is used with a mouse to bring additional lines of information into view in a window or list box.

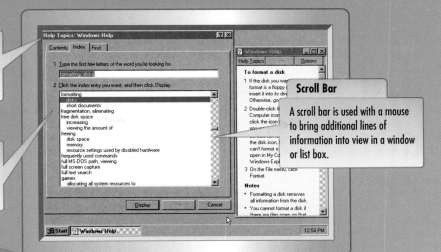

Formatting a Disk

Formatting converts a new disk from a generic state into a format your computer can use.

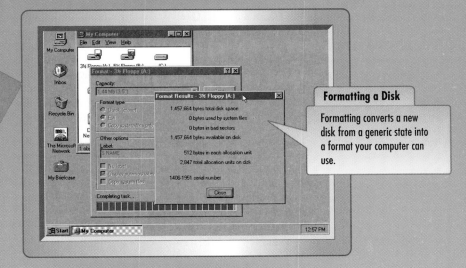

Menus

You enter instructions for the computer by choosing commands from menus.

Status Bar

The status bar displays information about current program settings and the task being performed.

Properties

All items on the screen have settings and attributes, called properties, associated with them.

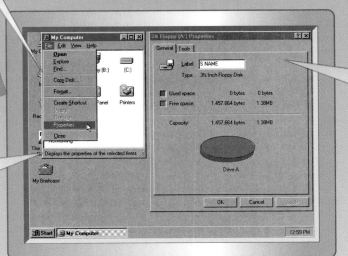

Windows 95 Disk Organization

Organizational skills are very important skills in any profession. When you are disorganized, it takes much longer to complete tasks accurately. Many Windows 95 features are aimed at making it easier for you to work effectively by helping you organize your work.

In this lab you will learn about many of Windows 95's organizational features. You will organize files into related categories, and display files in many different ways, making it easy to quickly locate files. You will arrange windows on the desktop to make it easier to view and work with information. In addition, many other file management features and shortcuts that will improve your efficiency will be introduced.

Concept Overview

The following concepts will be introduced in this lab:

1. Files and Folders
The information on your computer is stored as files. Folders contain files that are related.

2. Toolbar
The toolbar contains buttons that are shortcuts for many of the most common menu commands.

3. Arranging Windows
Windows can be arranged in two ways on the desktop, Cascade and Tile.

4. Undo
The Undo feature allows you to reverse your last action or command.

5. Hierarchy of Folders
The organization of folders, subfolders, and files on your disk is called a hierarchy or tree.

6. Cut, Copy, and Paste
All Windows applications include features that allow you to remove (cut), duplicate (copy), and insert (paste) information from one location to another.

7. File and Folder Names
Both files and folders are assigned names that are descriptive of the contents of the file or folder.

8. Drag and Drop
Common to all Windows applications is the ability to copy or move selections by dragging and dropping.

Part 1

Using My Computer to View Files and Folders

Turn on the computer. If necessary, close the Welcome window.

Information is stored as files on the computer's hard disk or on a floppy disk. A disk can hold many files of different types. To make it easy to locate files, you can store related files in folders. The My Computer window is used to view the files, folders, and other items that are on your computer.

Concept 1: Files and Folders

The information your computer uses is stored in a variety of different types of **files**. Two of the most common are program and data files. Instructions to run a program are stored in program files. For example, the word processing program on your computer consists of many files that contain the program statements required to use the program. The information you create while using a program is stored in data files. For example, if you write a letter to a friend using the word processing program, the contents of the letter are stored as a data file.

In addition, you can create **folders** and **subfolders** in which you store files that are related. Storing related files in folders keeps the disk organized and makes it much easier to locate files. Both files and folders are identified by names that are descriptive of the contents of the file or folder.

In many operating systems, folders are called directories.

OPERATING SYSTEM

Open the My Computer window.
Your screen should be similar to Figure 2-1.

drive icons

Figure 2-1

My Computer window

My Computer button   system folder icons

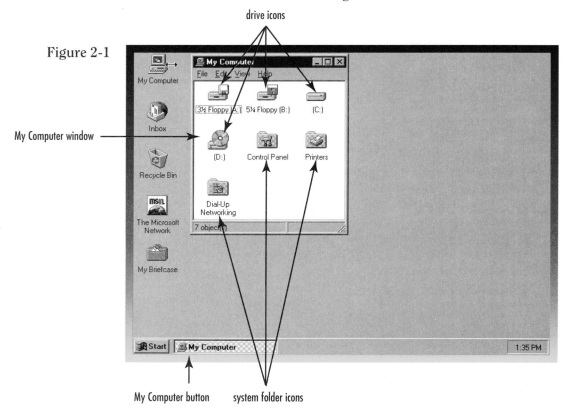

The My Computer window is open, and the taskbar displays the button for the window. The window size and placement on your desktop may be different than in Figure 2-1. This is because Windows 95 displays the window as it appeared when last used.

The My Computer window displays icons that reflect the setup of your computer system. The drive icons represent the drives on your computer system. In addition, the window displays system folder icons. The [Control Panel] Control Panel folder contains additional icons that are used to modify Windows 95 settings, and the [Printers] Printers folder contains icons that are used to modify the printer settings.

Selecting a drive icon displays the contents of the disk in that drive. To see the contents of your computer's hard drive,

Double-click: [C:]   (or the appropriate hard drive for your system)

A second window is open, and the taskbar displays the button for this window. The window displays file folder icons [ ], which represent the folders on the hard disk. The folder name appears to the right of each folder icon. The folders are displayed in alphabetical order.

Locate the Windows folder.

> Do not be concerned if the icons in your My Computer window are displayed differently than in Figure 2-1. You will learn about how to change the icon display shortly.

> You may need to scroll the window to see the Windows folder.

To see the contents of this folder,

Double-click: 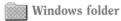 **Windows folder**

Your screen should be similar to Figure 2-2.

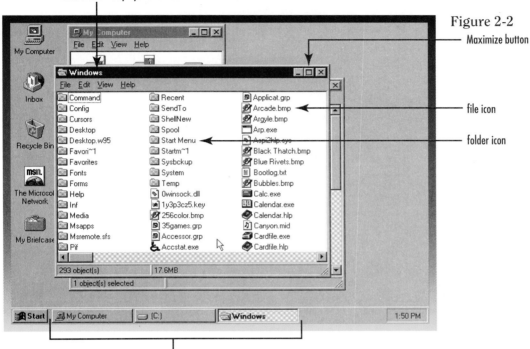

third window displays contents of Windows folder

Figure 2-2

Maximize button

file icon

folder icon

three taskbar buttons representing three open windows

A third window appears, and a third button is displayed in the taskbar. Each time you open an item while in My Computer, the contents of the item appear in a new window and a new button appears in the taskbar.

The Windows folder window contains many other folders. Again, do not be concerned if the display of the icons in this window is different than in Figure 2-2. You will learn how to change the appearance of the window next.

Maximize the Windows folder window.

In addition, you will see many other kinds of icons that represent files on your disk. Files follow folders in the list and also appear in alphabetical order by name. The different file icons represent different types of files. The various file icons help you distinguish the type of file: a program file, an associated file, or another type of file (generally a nonassociated document file). An **associated file** is a file that has a specific application program attached to it that will open when the file is opened. The table below describes several of the file icons.

Icon	Kind of File
	Represents program (executable) files and batch files
	Represents a Microsoft Word document file
	Represents a Lotus 1-2-3 worksheet file
	Represents a bitmap file
	Represents a Help file
	Represents document files that are not associated with an application

Changing the Window View

Items in a window can be viewed or displayed in four different ways. These views change the icon size, display order, and the amount of information about the files and folders. Depending upon what you are doing, one view may be more helpful than another.

The View menu contains the commands to change views. In addition, many of these commands have toolbar button shortcuts that can be used instead of selecting from the menu.

Concept 2: Toolbar

The **toolbar** is a bar of buttons that is commonly displayed below the menu bar. The buttons are shortcuts for many of the most common menu commands. The picture in the button is a graphic representation of the task the button activates. The buttons that appear in the toolbar vary with the application that is open in the window. All of the My Computer windows display the toolbar shown below.

If the toolbar is not displayed, you need to turn it on. To do this,

Choose: V̲iew

The View menu commands are used to customize the appearance of the window. To turn on the display of the toolbar,

A ✔ checkmark or a ● bullet next to a command indicates the feature is on.

Choose: T̲oolbar

If necessary, in a similar manner, display the status bar.

Your screen should be similar to Figure 2-3.

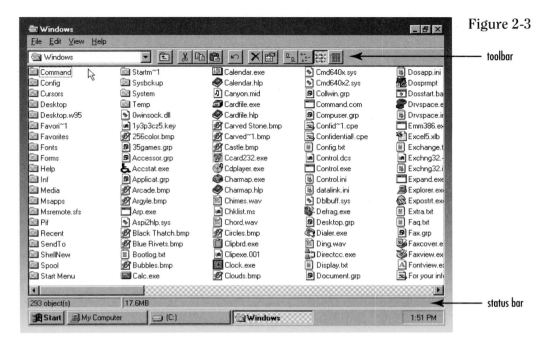

Figure 2-3

— toolbar

— status bar

Although the toolbar button icons represent specific features, it is often difficult to know what each button does. To find out the function of a button, you can display the button name. To do this, rest the mouse pointer over the button, and a **Tooltip** displaying a description of the button will appear.

Point to each toolbar button and read the related Tooltip.

Next you will change the window to display the information in several different views. To set the view to display the icons as large icons,

Click:  **Large Icons**

The menu equivalent is <u>V</u>iew/<u>L</u>arge Icons.

Your screen should be similar to Figure 2-4.

Large Icons button

Figure 2-4

alphabetically arranged
across rows

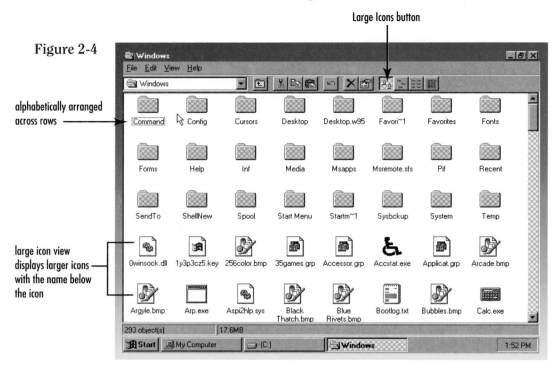

large icon view
displays larger icons
with the name below
the icon

The icons are large, with the icon name displayed below the icon. They appear in alphabetical order from left to right across the window. Notice that the Large Icons toolbar button appears depressed. This indicates the current view.

Another view is Small Icons. To see how this changes the display,

The menu equivalent is <u>V</u>iew/S<u>m</u>all Icons.

Click:  **Small Icons**

Your screen should be similar to Figure 2-5.

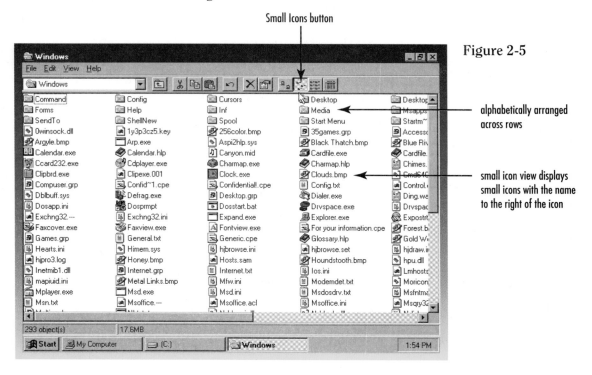

Figure 2-5

Small Icons button

alphabetically arranged across rows

small icon view displays small icons with the name to the right of the icon

The information is displayed in the same order, but many more folders and files can be displayed because the icon size is much smaller. The icon name appears to the right of the icon.

The next view, List, is similar to the Small Icons view.

Click: List

The menu equivalent is View/List.

The icons are the same size as in Small Icon view, but they are arranged alphabetically down columns rather than across rows in the window.

The last view setting displays the file details, such as total file size, type, and date and time of creation. To see this view,

Click: Details

The menu equivalent is View/Details.

Your screen should be similar to Figure 2-6.

Figure 2-6

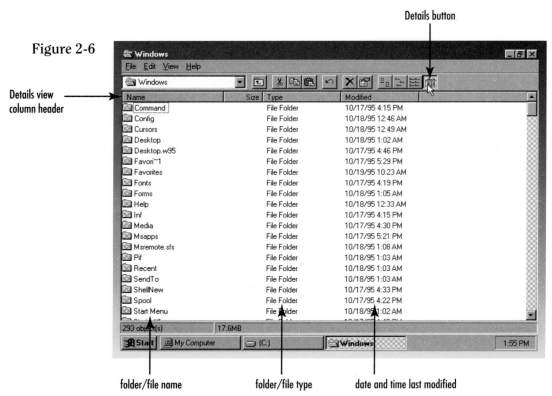

Details button

Details view
column header

folder/file name   folder/file type   date and time last modified

The names of the folders and files appear in a single column down the window, with the additional file information displayed in columns to the right. The columns are labeled with a column header. The columns display the file or folder name, the file size (in bytes), type of file, and date and time the file was last modified.

If necessary, scroll the window to see the file icons.

This additional information takes up a lot of space in the window, making it necessary to scroll the window to locate a file or folder that is not visible. Rather than use this view to see the file's details, you can display the details for an individual file by viewing the file's properties. To see how this works, you will change the view back to List. Another way to change the view is to select the command from the folder shortcut menu. This method is useful if the toolbar is not displayed.

> Right-click on the window background, not a folder or file, to display the folder shortcut menu.

Using the folder window shortcut menu, return the view to List.

Now, to view the properties of a file, select any file from the list.

Click: 📄 **Properties**

> The menu equivalent is File/Properties or Properties from the file's shortcut menu. You can also hold down [Alt] while double-clicking the filename to display the Properties box.

Depending upon the type of file you selected, the Properties tab dialog box may display the General tab and the Version tab. The Version tab only appears if the file type is a program file.

If necessary, open the General tab.

Your screen should be similar to Figure 2-7.

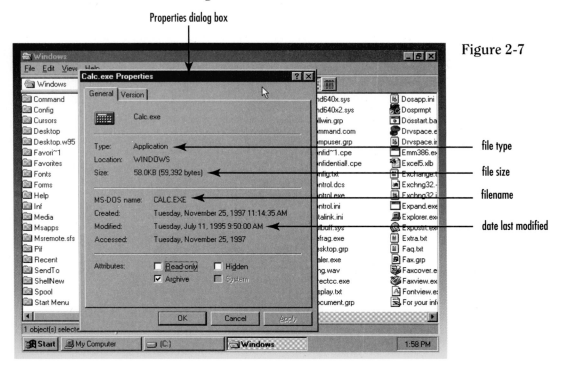

Properties dialog box

Figure 2-7

file type

file size

filename

date last modified

The General tab displays the same information as in Details view, such as file size and date for the selected file, plus some additional information.

After looking at the property information, close the dialog box.

Arranging Icons

Regardless of the view you are using, folders always appear first as a group, followed by files. Typically, folders and files are displayed in alphabetical order by name. Sometimes, however, this order is not convenient. For example, you may be unable to remember the name of the file, but you can remember the date you last modified it. The Arrange Icons command in the View menu lets you select an arrangement that may be more convenient for the task you are performing.

To arrange the files by size rather than name,

Choose: **View/Arrange Icons/by Size**

To verify that the files are in ascending order by file size, change the view to Details and scroll the window, looking at the Size column of information.

Your screen should be similar to Figure 2-8.

files arranged in ascending order by size

Figure 2-8

column heads ──────→

Name	Size	Type	Modified
hipro3.log	2KB	LOG File	11/4/95 1:06 PM
System.ini	2KB	Configuration Settings	11/26/97 11:50 PM
Msfntmap.ini	2KB	Configuration Settings	7/20/95 12:00 AM
Dblbuff.sys	3KB	System file	7/11/95 9:50 AM
Control.exe	3KB	Application	7/11/95 9:50 AM
Bubbles.bmp	3KB	Bitmap Image	7/11/95 9:50 AM
telephon.ini	3KB	Configuration Settings	11/25/97 11:29 AM
hipro.set	3KB	SET File	11/25/97 10:19 AM
wpcfg61.reg	3KB	Registration Entries	10/19/95 12:46 PM
Winhelp.exe	3KB	Application	7/11/95 9:50 AM
Multimed.grp	3KB	Microsoft Program Gr...	11/25/97 12:36 PM
Extra.txt	3KB	Text Document	7/11/95 9:50 AM
Internet.grp	3KB	Microsoft Program Gr...	11/25/97 12:36 PM
Red Blocks.bmp	3KB	Bitmap Image	7/11/95 9:50 AM
Internet.txt	4KB	Text Document	7/11/95 9:50 AM
Win.---	4KB	--- File	4/25/95 2:47 PM
touchup.ini	4KB	Configuration Settings	11/10/95 8:42 PM
wpdraw30.reg	4KB	Registration Entries	10/19/95 12:46 PM
Winver.exe	4KB	Application	7/11/95 9:50 AM
Lmhosts.sam	4KB	SAM File	7/11/95 9:50 AM

1 object(s) selected   58.0KB

Start   My Computer   (C:)   Windows   2:01 PM

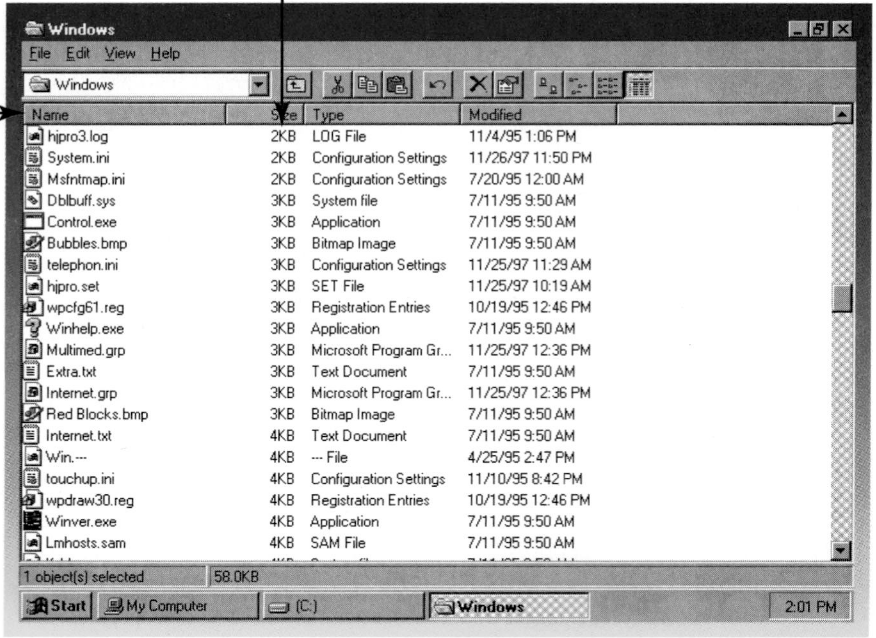

> Because folders do not include a size, they remain at the top of the list in alphabetical order.

The order can also be changed to display by date or by file type (according to the file extension). Usually, the most useful view is by name.

Another way to change the display order when using Details view is to click the column heads. For example, clicking the Name column head changes the display order back to ascending alphabetical order by filename. Clicking the column head of a selected order switches between ascending and descending order. To change the order back to display the files by filename,

> The menu equivalent is View/Arrange Icons/ by Name.

Click: Name

Return the view to List view.

Switching Between Windows

Next you would like to see the contents of your newly formatted data disk.

Put the disk you formatted in Lab 1 in the appropriate drive.

To view the disk's contents, you need to return to the My Computer window to select the drive icon that contains your disk. However, you cannot see the window on your desktop because it is covered by the Windows folder window. To bring the My Computer window to the forefront,

> 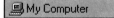 is in the taskbar.

Click: My Computer

The My Computer window becomes the active window and it appears on top of the other windows. It is easy to tell which window on the screen is active. Active windows are displayed on top, have colored title bars, and their buttons are depressed in the taskbar.

Double-click: (or the drive containing your formatted disk)

Your screen should be similar to Figure 2-9.

> Drive A will be used throughout the text. If you are using another drive, select the appropriate drive for your system.

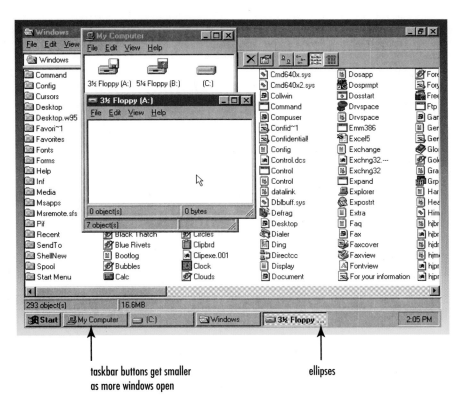

Figure 2-9

taskbar buttons get smaller
as more windows open

ellipses

The drive window is open and displayed on top of the other windows. It is the active window. Because the disk is newly formatted, the window does not display any files or folder objects.

There are now four buttons displayed in the taskbar along with four windows open on the desktop. You can switch to any window you can see on the desktop simply by clicking on it.

Click on the Windows folder window to make it active, restore the window to its original size, then minimize the window.

Now there are three displayed windows on the desktop. However, there are still four buttons in the taskbar. Notice that as more windows are opened on the desktop, the taskbar buttons get smaller to allow all buttons to be displayed on the taskbar. This shortens the amount of text in the button and makes it difficult to know which button is which. Ellipses following the button name indicate the name has been shortened. Pointing to the button will display the complete window name in a Tooltip box.

> Point to the floppy-disk button to see the Tooltip.

Another way to see more of the button identification is to make the taskbar larger, just like you would a window.

> Drag the upper border of the taskbar upward.

Your screen should be similar to Figure 2-10.

> The taskbar can also be moved just like a window.

Figure 2-10

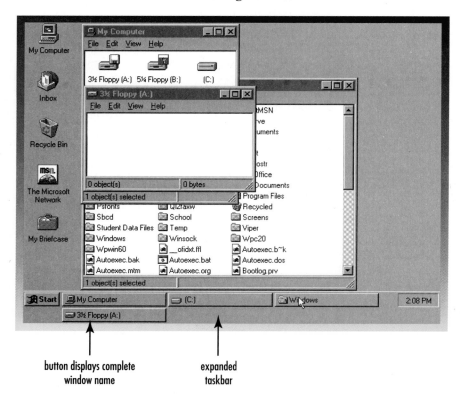

button displays complete
window name

expanded
taskbar

The taskbar now displays two lines, allowing more space for the buttons, and the window name is fully displayed.

Arranging Windows

As you can see, as more windows are open on the desktop, it is harder to see the information in the windows. To make viewing of multiple windows easier, you could move and size windows as you learned to do in Lab 1. Another way is to use built-in windows arranging features.

Concept 3: Arranging Windows

There are two ways to arrange windows on the desktop: Cascade and Tile.

Cascade	Layers open windows, displaying the active window fully and only the title bars of all other open windows behind it
Tile	Resizes each open window and arranges the windows vertically or horizontally on the desktop

Cascading windows is useful if you want to work primarily in one window but you want to see the titles of other open windows. Tiling is most useful when you want to work in several applications simultaneously, because it allows you to quickly see the contents of all open windows and move between them. However, the more windows that are open, the smaller is the space available to display the tiled window contents.

The taskbar shortcut menu displays options that allow you to arrange windows.

Right-click on any blank area of the taskbar to display its shortcut menu.

To cascade the three open windows,

Choose: **C**ascade

Your screen should be similar to Figure 2-11.

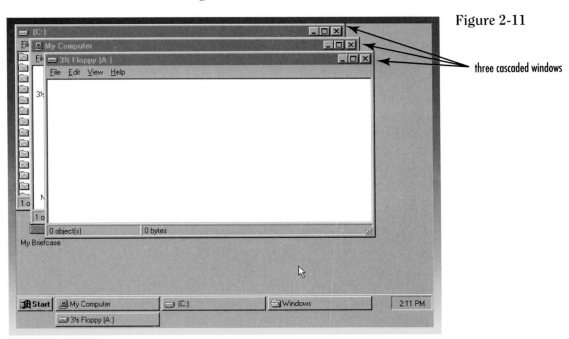

Figure 2-11

three cascaded windows

The windows are resized and overlap with the title bars visible. Only open windows that are not minimized are arranged.

You can click on any visible part of the window to make it active.
Make the My Computer window active.

The My Computer window is now active. It is pulled to the front of the stack and covers the other cascaded windows. Depending on how the windows overlap, you may need to use the taskbar buttons to make a window that is no longer visible active, or use the Cascade command again to rearrange the windows in cascade order.

As you switch between windows, it becomes more difficult to see the title bars. To restore the window size and arrangement as it was prior to cascading the windows, you can use the Undo command.

Concept 4: Undo

The Undo feature allows you to reverse your last action or command. However, some actions you perform in Windows cannot be undone. If the Undo command is unavailable, it appears dimmed and you cannot cancel your last action. Some programs allow you to undo multiple actions, up to a certain limit. This command is found on the Edit menu. The shortcut key is Ctrl + Z and the toolbar button is ☜. It is also on many Shortcut menus. Undo is selected from the menu or toolbar in the window in which the action you want to undo was performed.

Display the Taskbar shortcut menu.

Notice that the shortcut menu now displays an Undo Cascade command. The Undo option appears only after windows have been arranged. Because the commands to arrange windows are in the taskbar shortcut menu, this is also the location of the command to undo window arrangement. From the taskbar shortcut menu,

Choose: <u>U</u>ndo Cascade

The windows are arranged and sized again as they were before using the Cascade command. If you do not undo the arrangement before switching to another arrangement, the windows remain in the size and position set by the second arrangement and cannot be returned to their original size without custom sizing and moving the windows.

To arrange the three windows on the desktop without overlapping, from the taskbar shortcut menu,

Choose: Tile <u>V</u>ertically

The three windows are vertically arranged on the desktop, each taking up one third of the vertical space. The minimized window is not included in the arrangement.

Display the Windows folder window.

Check the taskbar button to display the window.

Your screen should be similar to Figure 2-12.

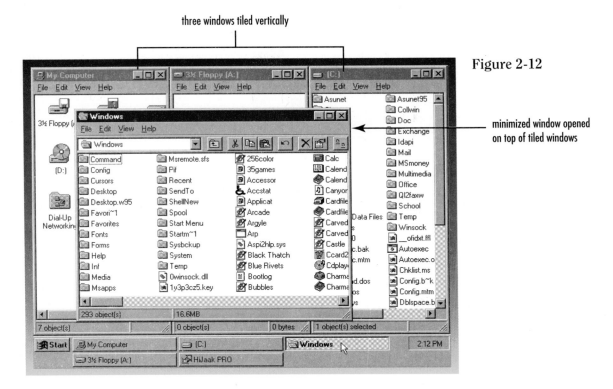

Figure 2-12

The window is opened on top of the three arranged windows. The program does not automatically arrange new windows as they are opened on the desktop.
Minimize the Windows folder window again.

Again, the tile arrangement can be reversed using the Undo command. From the taskbar shortcut menu,

Choose: Undo tile

Then, to tile the open windows horizontally, from the taskbar shortcut menu,

Choose: Tile Horizontally

Your screen should be similar to Figure 2-13.

Figure 2-13

three windows
tiled horizontally

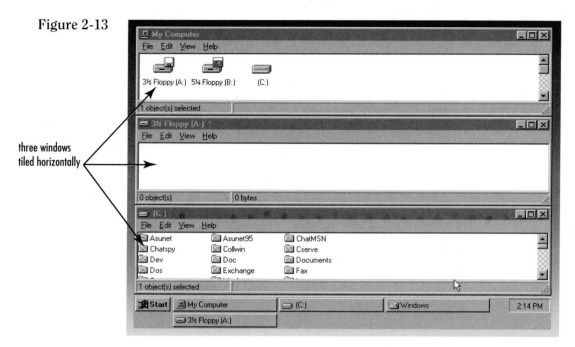

Undo this arrangement.

Finally, the taskbar shortcut menu also allows you to quickly minimize all open windows. From the taskbar shortcut menu,

Choose: **Minimize All Windows**

The desktop is cleared of all open windows. This is much quicker than minimizing each window individually.

Closing Minimized Windows

When a window is minimized, it can be closed by using the Close command on the button's shortcut menu. First you will close the Windows folder window.

Display the shortcut menu for the Windows folder taskbar button.

Choose: <u>C</u>lose

The window is closed, and the button no longer appears in the taskbar. The shortcut to close the active windows is [Alt] + [F4]. However, when all windows are minimized, using this shortcut quits the Windows 95 program, closing all open windows for you.

Since you do not want to quit yet, close the other three open windows using the Close command.

Resize the taskbar to its original size by dragging the top border down.

Note: If you are ending your lab session now, quit Windows 95.

Part 2

Using Explorer

Windows **Explorer** is another application included in Windows 95 that helps you view and organize the files on your disk. You can start the Windows Explorer application in many different ways. One way is to select the command from the File menu in the My Computer window. The shortcut for this is to use the My Computer shortcut menu, eliminating the need to open the My Computer window first.

Display the My Computer shortcut menu.

The My Computer shortcut menu displays the commonly used commands in the My Computer window. To open the Windows Explorer,

Choose: <u>E</u>xplore

The Exploring window is displayed.

If necessary, maximize the window, use the View menu to turn on the toolbar and status bar, and change the view to Large Icons.

Your screen should be similar to Figure 2-14 on the following page. The title bar displays the name of the application, and the menu bar displays five menus. The menus contain many of the same commands as in My Computer. In addition, the toolbar displays the same buttons.

Read the information in the Parts of the Exploring Window box on the next page for a description of this window.

Parts of the Exploring Window

Figure 2-14

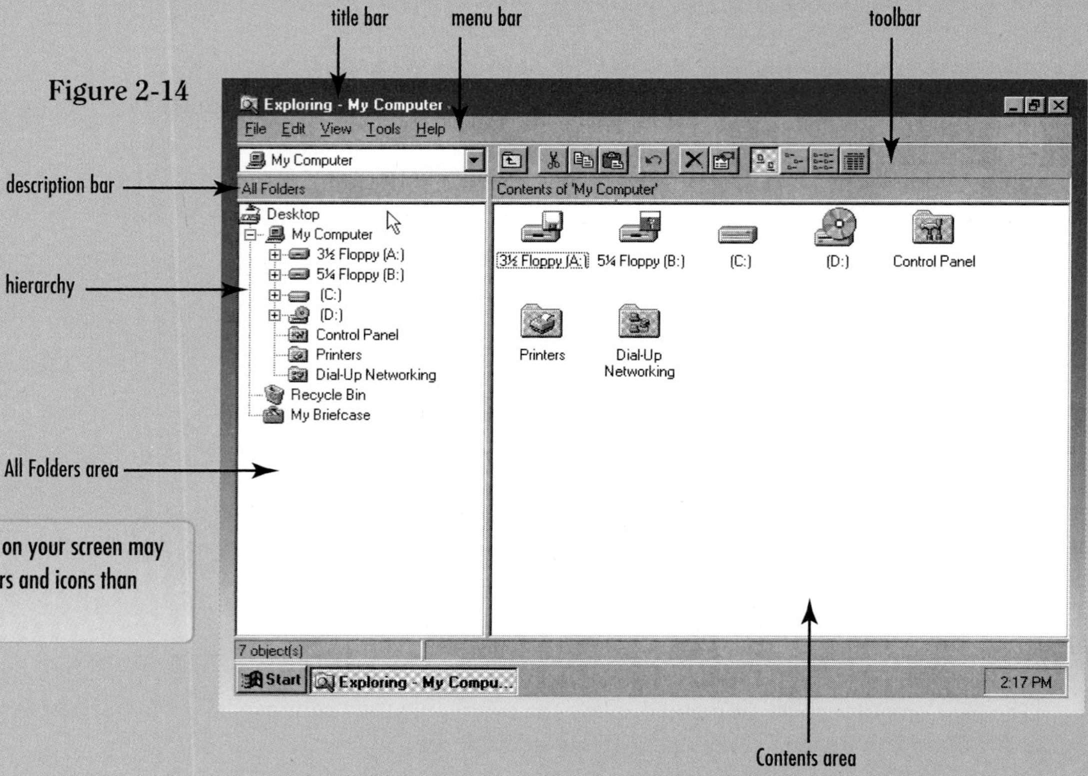

title bar   menu bar   toolbar

description bar

hierarchy

All Folders area

The Exploring window on your screen may display different folders and icons than those in Figure 2-14.

Contents area

You can change the size of either area by dragging the bar that separates the two areas.

The Exploring window is divided into two areas. The **description bar** above each area identifies the area content. The left area is the **All Folders area**, which shows a graphic representation of the organization of the major parts of your computer.

The right area, called the **Contents area**, displays the contents of the selected item in the All Folders area. In this case, because you opened Windows Explorer from the My Computer shortcut menu, the Contents area shows icons for the drives on your computer and the same folders as in the My Computer window. The description bar identifies the contents that are currently displayed in the area.

The graphic representation of the organization of the disk displayed in the All Folders area is called a hierarchy or tree.

Concept 5: Hierarchy of Folders

The organization of folders, subfolders, and files on your disk is displayed as a **hierarchy** or **tree**. The top-level folder of a disk is the **main folder**. On the hard disk, the main folder is represented by the Desktop icon (see Figure 2-15). On a floppy disk, the main folder is represented by the drive icon. This folder is created when the disk is formatted. The leftmost vertical line is the main tree line. On the hard disk it includes all items that appear on the desktop (under the Desktop icon). All folders are branches from the main folder. Subfolders are branches under a folder. Files can be stored in the main folder, a folder, or a subfolder.

Selecting a different item in the All Folders area displays the contents of the selected item in the Contents area. To see the contents of the hard drive,

Click: ▭ (C:) **(or the appropriate drive for your system)**

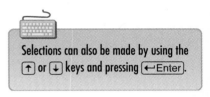

Selections can also be made by using the ↑ or ↓ keys and pressing ←Enter.

Your screen should be similar to Figure 2-15.

main tree line   selected item   contents of drive C
main folder

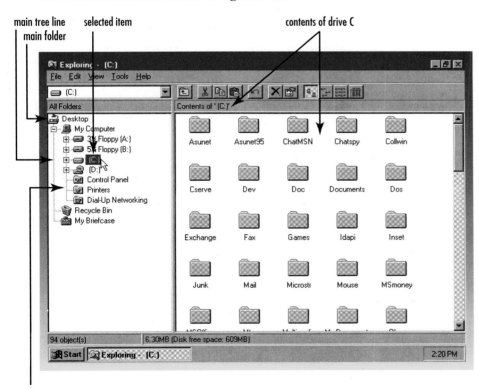

Figure 2-15

branch

The selection cursor (the dotted blue rectangle surrounding the text) appears over the selected item in the All Folders area.

The Contents area on your screen will reflect the folders and files on your computer's hard drive.

The Contents area displays the contents of the selected item. The Contents area description bar indicates the area is displaying the contents of the C drive. If the drive contains folders, they are displayed first, in alphabetical order, followed by the files.

You can also display the folders in the All Folders area of the window. To do this, you click the ⊞ sign that is displayed to the left of the drive icon to expand the hierarchy. To display the folders on your hard drive,

Click: ⊞ **beside your hard drive icon**

Your screen should be similar to Figure 2-16.

Figure 2-16

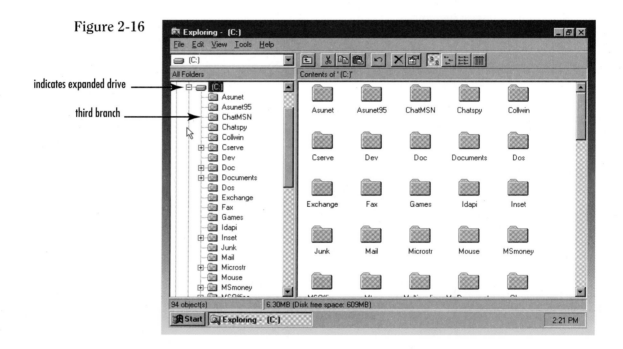

indicates expanded drive

third branch

The All Folders area displays the folders on your hard drive as a third branch on the hierarchy. Notice that the ⊞ changed to a ⊟ , which shows that the drive icon is fully open or expanded.

Clicking the ⊟ sign or double-clicking an expanded folder hides the folders again in the All Folders area.

You can also expand a folder that contains subfolders. The ⊞ appears next to a folder only if it contains subfolders. Another way to expand the hierarchy display is by double-clicking the folder or drive icon. To expand the Windows folder,

You may need to scroll the All Folders area to see the Windows folder icon.

Double-click: **Windows**

The selection cursor highlights the folder name, the Windows folder icon appears open 🗁, indicating the folder is open, and the ⊟ symbol indicates it is expanded. The folders in the Windows folder appear as a fourth branch on the hierarchy. As you select items in the All Folders area, the Contents area displays the folders and files in the selected item.

The same information you viewed by opening multiple windows using My Computer is displayed in one window using Explorer. Fewer windows makes it much easier to view and manage the information, and as you will see, it makes it very easy to copy and move folders and files from one disk or folder to another.

Copying Files

Now that you know how to browse your computer to locate folders and files, you will copy the files needed to complete this lab (and others your instructor may be using) to your newly formatted data disk.

Concept 6: Cut, Copy, and Paste

All Windows applications include features that allow you to remove (**cut**), duplicate (**copy**), and insert (**paste**) information from one location to another. The commands to perform these tasks are found in the Edit menu and on the toolbar. The information must be selected before it is copied or cut. The location that contains the information you want to cut or copy is called the **source**. Then the command to cut or copy the selection is used, and the selection is stored in a temporary storage area in memory called the **Clipboard**. Finally, you select the location, called the **destination**, where you want to insert a copy of the information stored in the Clipboard, and then you use the Paste command.

You will learn more about the Clipboard in Lab 3.

This text assumes the files are in a folder named "Student Data Files" on your hard drive. If your school uses a different folder name or your computer is on a network and the data files are in a folder on another system disk, your instructor will provide additional instructions.

The files you will copy should be in a folder on your hard disk. First you need to open the folder containing the data files.

Open the Student Data Files folder (or the folder containing your data files).

The subfolders contained in your Student Data Files folder are displayed in the Contents area.

Expand the Student Data Files folder.

The folders should now appear in the hierarchy in the All Folders area.

Open the Windows 95 folder.

The data files you will need to complete the Windows 95 lab are displayed in alphabetical order by filename in the Contents area (see Figure 2-17 on the next page).

Next you will select the files you want to copy to your floppy disk. When you copy a file from one location to another, you first need to select the file you want to copy from the Contents area.

Click: anywhere in the Contents area

Your screen should be similar to Figure 2-17.

Contents area displays data
files for Windows 95 labs

Figure 2-17

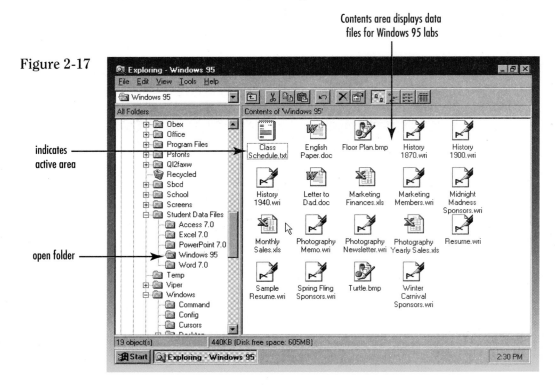

indicates
active area

open folder

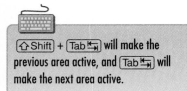

⟨⬆Shift⟩ + ⟨Tab ⇆⟩ will make the
previous area active, and ⟨Tab ⇆⟩ will
make the next area active.

If you clicked on a file, the file icon is selected (highlighted). If you clicked on an open area, a dotted box appears around the name of the first file in the list. The highlight no longer appears in the All Folders area. Whichever area contains the dotted box or highlight is the **active area**, or the area that will be affected by the next action you perform. Clicking anywhere in either area makes it the active area.

First you will copy the file named Class Schedule. To select this file,

Click:

Class
Schedule.txt

Your screen should be similar to Figure 2-18.

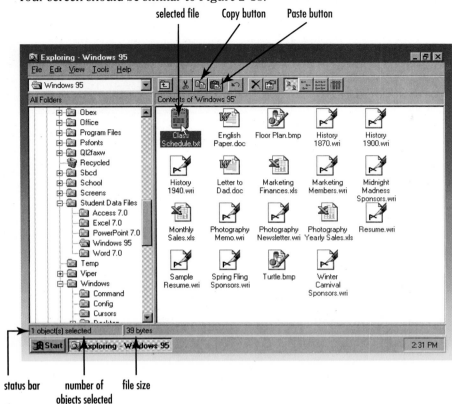

Figure 2-18

The selection cursor appears over the selected file icon. The status bar indicates one object is selected and its size. To copy the file,

Click: 📋 Copy

When you use the Copy command, a copy of the selected item, in this case the file, is stored in the Clipboard. Now you need to tell Windows 95 where you want the file copied to by specifying the destination. Your destination will be the disk in the floppy drive. To select the destination, you need to make the All Folders area active and select the drive containing your data disk.

Make the All Folders area active.

Select: 💾 3½ Floppy (A:)

The Contents area is empty because there are no files or folders on this disk yet. The Paste command is used to insert the copy of the information, which is stored in the Clipboard, in the selected destination.

Click: 📋 Paste

A Copying message box is displayed as the file is copied.

Your screen should be similar to Figure 2-19.

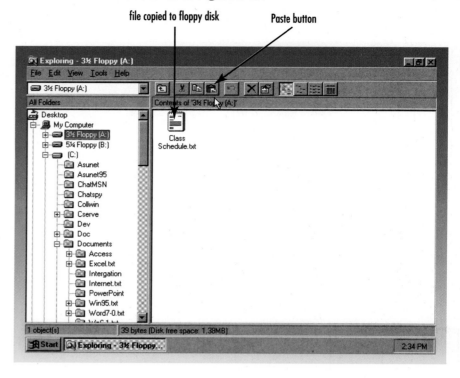

Figure 2-19

The Contents area is updated, and the Class Schedule file icon is displayed. The file was copied to the main folder of the floppy disk (this folder was created when the disk was formatted). You are now ready to copy the rest of the files to your data disk.

Select the Windows 95 folder in the All Folders area again.

Notice that the Class Schedule file is still displayed in the Windows 95 Contents area. Because you copied the file, it is now in both the Windows 95 folder and on your data disk.

Using Send To

Next you need to copy the other Windows 95 data files to the main folder of your data disk. Instead of using copy and paste, you can use the Send To command on the File menu. This command makes the process easier by allowing you to copy files directly to the main folder of a destination disk without having to select it first.

Rather than select and copy each file individually, you will select all the files in the folder and copy them at the same time.

Make the Contents area active.

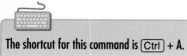

The shortcut for this command is ⌈Ctrl⌉ + A.

Choose: Edit/Select All

All the file icons in the folder are selected. To quickly copy the files to the disk in the floppy drive,

Choose: F̲ile/Sen̲d To

A submenu listing the drives you can copy the files to is displayed. To select the drive where you want the copied files sent,

Select: 🖼 3½ Floppy (A:)

The Copying message box is displayed as the files are copied. In addition, because the Class Schedule file is already on the disk in drive A, a Confirm File Replace dialog box appears. Windows 95 displays this message so you do not accidentally overwrite one file with another of the same name.

Your screen should be similar to Figure 2-20.

> The Send To command is also on the selected objects shortcut menu.

Copying message box   Go to a Different
                       Folder button   Confirm File Replace dialog box

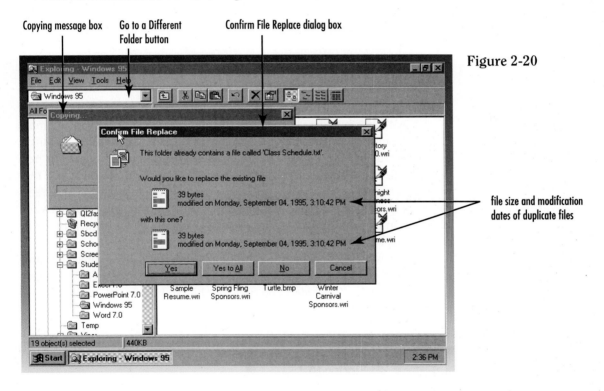

Figure 2-20

file size and modification
dates of duplicate files

The dialog box shows the size of the duplicate files and date and time the files were last modified. Because you just copied the Class Schedule file, you can overwrite it without changing its contents, or you can choose No to bypass this operation and continue. To bypass copying this file again,

Choose: N̲o

There are no other duplicate files, and all the files have been copied to the main folder of your data disk.

To view the contents of your data disk, you could select the drive icon from the All Folders area as you did previously. However, when the disk contains a large number of folders, this requires scrolling the area. A quicker way to change locations is to use the Go to a Different Folder button on the toolbar, shown in Figure 2-20 on the previous page. This type of button is called a drop-down list button. It consists of two parts: a text box that displays the current selection, in this case the selected folder, and a button. Clicking the button displays a drop-down list of options.

Click:

A brief version of the disk hierarchy is displayed. To switch to the drive containing your data disk,

Select: ⬜ 3½ Floppy (A:)

The Contents area displays the 19 files that were copied from the source to your data disk.

Creating Folders

Now that you have learned how Windows organizes folders and files, you will learn how to create folders to organize the files on your disk. As you add more files to the main folder of a disk, it gets very crowded and disorganized. This is especially true of hard disks, which can hold large amounts of data. To help organize files into like categories, you can create folders. For example, you may want to store software programs and the files you create using these programs by the program type. Alternatively, you might want to store your programs and information by project. You can create further divisions within each folder by creating additional subfolders.

Currently the files on your disk are simply alphabetically arranged by name in the main folder on the disk. You will create folders for the related files to help organize your disk. The folders and subfolder hierarchy you will create is shown in Figure 2-21.

Figure 2-21

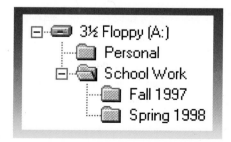

The first folder you will create on your data disk will be used to hold school-related documents. The command to create a folder is New on the File menu. To indicate where you want the folder created, the destination location must be selected first. Since the drive containing your data disk is already selected, you are ready to create the folder.

Choose: File/New/Folder

Your screen should be similar to Figure 2-22.

Figure 2-22

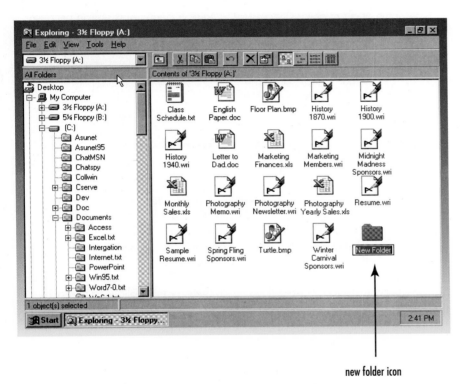

new folder icon

A folder icon is displayed in the Contents area, with the temporary folder name of New Folder highlighted. Notice the insertion point displayed at the end of the folder name. This indicates that Windows 95 is waiting for you to replace the default name with a descriptive name for the folder you are creating.

Concept 7: File and Folder Names

File and folder names are used to identify the contents of a file or folder. The name you assign a folder or file must be unique for the folder it is in. For example, if you give a new file the same name as an existing file in the same folder, the contents of the original file will be replaced by the contents of the new file. Many software programs have safeguards to prevent accidentally overwriting one file with another. Folder names must also be unique.

In addition to a filename, a **filename extension** can be added. A filename extension is up to three characters and is separated from the filename by a period. Generally a filename extension is used to identify the type of file. It is not always necessary to enter a filename extension because most application programs automatically add an identifying filename extension to any files created using the program. For instance, Word 7.0 files have a filename extension of "doc." A folder extension is not generally used and is never supplied by the operating system.

The parts of a filename are shown below.

filename   filename extension

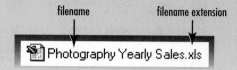

Windows 95 and programs that are designed to operate under Windows 95 allow you to use long folder and **filenames** of up to 255 characters. They can contain the letters A to Z, the numbers 0 to 9, and any of the following special characters: underscore (_), caret (^), dollar sign ($), tilde (~), exclamation point (!), number sign (#), percent sign (%), ampersand (&), hyphen (-), braces ({}), parentheses (), "at" sign (@), apostrophe ('), and the grave accent (`). Spaces are allowed in names, but the following characters are not allowed: \ / : * ? " < > |.

The restrictions regarding characters also apply to filename extensions.

Because this folder will be used to hold files related to your school work, you will name the new folder School Work. With the text "New Folder" highlighted,

Type: **School Work**

To complete the entry,

Press: ← Enter

The folder name appears exactly as you typed it (including case). The insertion point is no longer displayed, but the folder is still selected.

> If you make a typing error, use the ← Backspace key to delete the characters to the left of the insertion point.

Next you want to create another folder named Personal to hold your personal files. You also want this folder in the main folder.

Select the A drive icon in the All Folders area. Create a new folder named Personal.

Now that the disk in the drive contains folders, the drive icon in the All Folders area is preceded with a ⊞ .

Expand the A Floppy drive icon to display the folders in the All Folders area.

Your screen should be similar to Figure 2-23.

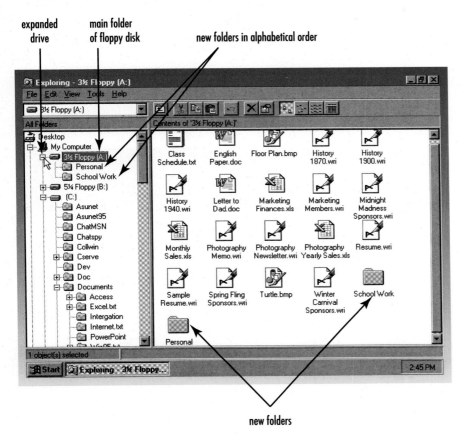

Figure 2-23

The two folders you created appear in alphabetical order in the All Folders area. However, the two new folders are not yet displayed in alphabetical order in the Contents area. To update the order of display of icons in the Contents area,

Choose: View/Arrange Icons/by Name

The folders now appear first in the Contents area and in alphabetical order.

Next you would like to further subdivide your files in the School Work folder by semesters: Fall 1997 and Spring 1998. To create a subfolder under the School folder, you must first select the School folder. When a folder is selected, it is the **current folder** or the folder you can work on. Only one folder can be current at a time.

Select the School Work folder in the All Folders area.

Notice that the Contents area is now blank. This is because there are no files or folders in the selected folder. The description bar displays "Contents of School Work."

Create a folder named Fall 1997.

The new folder is displayed in the School Contents area, and a ⊕ appears next to the School Work folder in the All Folders area to show that the folder contains a subfolder.

Next create the Spring 1998 subfolder in the School Work folder. (Make sure the School folder is selected first.)

The folder appears in the Contents area.

Then, to display the folders in the All Folders area, expand the School Work folder.

Your screen should be similar to Figure 2-24.

Figure 2-24

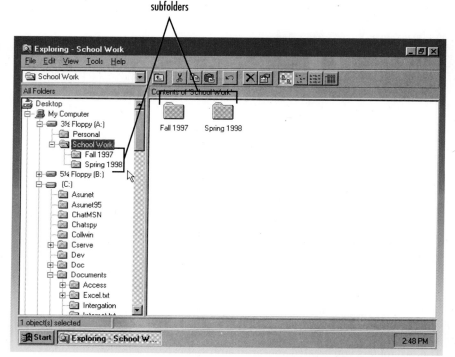

The two new folders are displayed under the School folder.

Copying a File to a Folder

Next you will copy a file from the main folder of your data disk into one of the folders you just created. You will copy the file Class Schedule into the School Work folder.

To select the file you want to copy, select the A drive icon in the All Folders area.

Select the Class Schedule icon in the Contents area.

Rather than using the Copy and Paste commands, you can use the drag and drop feature to copy a file.

Concept 8: Drag and Drop

Common to all Windows applications is the ability to copy or move selections using the **drag and drop** feature. After selecting the item to be copied or moved, pointing to it and dragging displays the drag and drop insertion point 🔲. The insertion point displays a + when copying will take place. Then dragging the mouse moves or copies the selection to the new location specified when you release the mouse button. The location you want to drag and drop to should be visible in the window.

If you drag a file to a folder on the same disk, it will be moved. If you drag a file to a folder on another disk, it will be copied. You can hold down ⇧Shift while dragging to always move a file, or Ctrl to copy a file. If you drag holding down the right mouse button, a shortcut menu appears with options to either copy or move the selection.

You will drag and drop the selected file icon from the Contents area to the School folder in the All Folders area.

With the mouse pointer on the selected file icon, hold down Ctrl and drag to the School Work folder in either area.

The mouse pointer appears as 🔲 while copying the file using drag and drop. When the pointer is positioned over the School Work folder and the folder is selected, release the mouse button and Ctrl.

The Copying message box appears while copying occurs. As you can see from the Contents area, the original file remains in the main folder. To verify that the file was copied,

A circle/slash symbol 🚫 is displayed when the mouse pointer is in an area where the file cannot be copied or moved.

Double-click: 📁 **School Work (in the Contents area)**

Your screen should be similar to Figure 2-25.

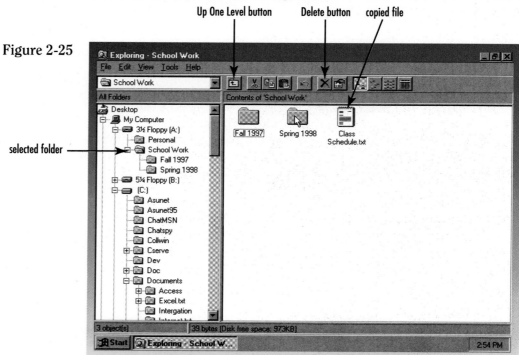

Up One Level button   Delete button   copied file

Figure 2-25

selected folder

The Contents area displays a file icon for the copied file.

Deleting Files

At some point, some of the files you have on your disk may no longer be needed and you will want to remove them from your disk to save space.

You will delete the Class Schedule file from the main folder now that you have a copy of it in the School Work folder. To quickly move up one level of the hierarchy to the main folder,

> You can also press ←Backspace to move back one level.

Click: Up One Level

Select the Class Schedule file icon in the Contents area.
To delete this file,

> You can also use the Delete command on the File or shortcut menus or the shortcut key Delete to delete a file or folder.

Click: ✖ Delete

> You will learn about the Recycle Bin in Lab 3.

The Confirm File Delete message box appears in which you must confirm that you want to remove the file. This is especially important when deleting files from a floppy disk, because they are permanently deleted. Files and folders that are deleted from the hard disk are not permanently deleted, but are placed in the Recycle Bin where they are held until they are permanently deleted from that location.

If you changed your mind, choosing No would cancel the procedure. To continue,

Choose: Yes

You cannot use Undo to reverse the action of deleting a file from a floppy disk.

Your screen should be similar to Figure 2-26.

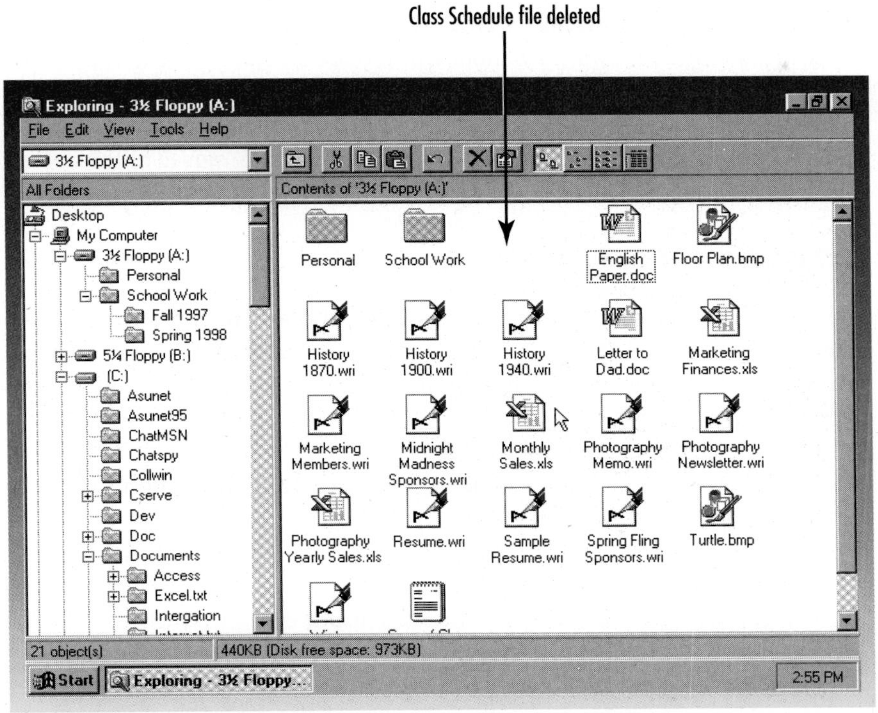

Class Schedule file deleted

Figure 2-26

The file is removed from the main folder of the disk, and its icon is no longer displayed in the Contents area.

Moving Files

Rather than copying and deleting files, you can **move** them from one location to another. First you would like to move the file English Paper to the School Work folder.

Select the English Paper file icon from the main folder of your data disk.

Files can be moved from one folder on a disk to another by using drag and drop.

Drag the English Paper file to the School Work folder in either area.

As the file is moved, the Moving message box is displayed. When the move is complete, the English Paper file icon is no longer displayed in the Contents area.

To see the file icon in the School Work folder, open the School Work folder.

You can also use the Cut and Paste commands on the Edit or shortcut menus or the toolbar buttons and to move a file.

The English Paper file icon is displayed in the folder. However, you decide you want this file to be in one of the subfolders of the School folder. It should really be in the Fall 1997 folder. To undo the move,

> The menu equivalent is Edit/Undo. The action that will be undone appears after the command name in the menu and Tooltip.

Click: **Undo**

The Moving dialog box is displayed again and the move is reversed. The English Paper file is removed from the School Work folder and placed back in the main folder.

Return to the main folder and move the English Paper file to the Fall 1997 folder. Open the Fall 1997 folder to verify that the file was moved to the correct location.

Extending a Selection

You can also select several files to copy or move at the same time. This is called **extending a selection**. You can quickly select several files that are scattered throughout the list, or several adjacent files. You can also select multiple groups of files from the list.

> Reminder: You can click 🗁 to move up a level.

Open the main folder of your data disk.

First you will move two nonadjacent files, Letter to Dad and Resume, to the Personal folder.

Select the Letter to Dad file icon.

The next file you will select is Resume.

If necessary, scroll the window until it is displayed.

To select a second file, you hold down Ctrl while clicking the file icon.

Hold down Ctrl.

Now, when you click on any other files, they will be selected (highlighted).

Select the Resume file icon.

> To deselect a file (remove the highlight), click on it again while holding down Ctrl.

If necessary, deselect any other files that you may have selected accidentally. Release Ctrl.

Your screen should be similar to Figure 2-27.

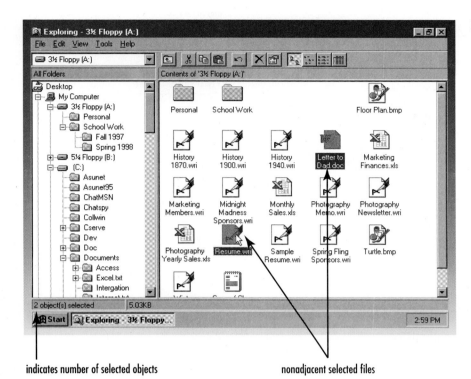

Figure 2-27

indicates number of selected objects   nonadjacent selected files

The two files are highlighted and the status bar indicates that two objects are selected.

> Move the files to the Personal folder.
>
> To verify that the files were moved, open the Personal folder.

Next you will select and copy a series of adjacent files from the main folder to the Fall 1997 folder of the School folder. The three files you want to copy are the three History files.

> Open the main folder of your data disk.

You will select the three adjacent files, History 1870 , History 1900, and History 1940. To do this you can hold down the mouse button and drag to create a box around the files. If a file you do not want selected is included in the box, holding down Ctrl while clicking the file deselects it, leaving all others selected. Likewise, you can add other files to the selection by holding down Ctrl while selecting them.

> Select the History 1870, History 1900, and History 1940 files by dragging a box around the file icons and adding or clearing selections as needed.
>
> Notice that the status bar indicates three objects are selected.
>
> Move the selected files to the Fall 1997 folder under the School Work folder.
>
> To verify that the files were moved to the destination folder, open the Fall 1997 folder.

> You can also use drag and drop with multiple files.

> Do not point to a file icon while dragging to create a box.

Your screen should be similar to Figure 2-28.

Figure 2-28

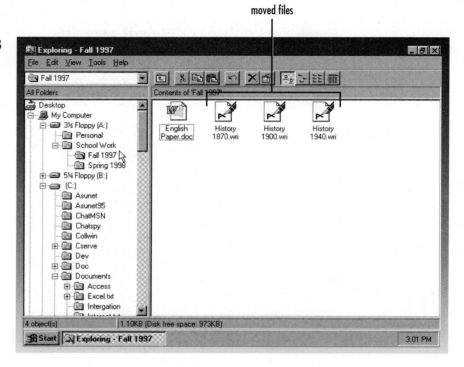

moved files

The file icons for the files you moved are displayed in the Contents area.

Renaming Files

Next, you want to change the name of the Class Schedule file in the School Work folder.

Make the School Work folder active.

This file actually contains the class schedules for the Fall 1997 semester only. You will rename this file Fall 1997 Class Schedule so that it is more descriptive of the information it contains.

Select: **Class Schedule**

To change the name of a file,

Choose: **File/Rename**

> You could also select the file icon and then click on the text area to display the insertion point and change the filename.

The filename appears highlighted and with an insertion point. To move the insertion point to the beginning of the filename,

Press: Ctrl + Home

The insertion point moves to the beginning of the filename, and the name is no longer selected. To add the semester in front of the filename,

Type: **Fall 1997**

To insert a space and complete the renaming,

Press: Spacebar
Press: ←Enter

The filename changes to its new name, Fall 1997 Class Schedule.

Deleting Folders

At some point, some of the folders you have on your disk may no longer be needed and you will want to remove them from your disk. As you learned earlier, to delete a file you select it, then use the Delete command to remove it. The same procedure is used to delete folders. In addition, when a folder is selected, using Delete will also remove all the files and subfolders contained within that folder.

Select the Personal folder in the All Folders area.

You will use the keyboard shortcut to delete the folder.

Press: Delete

The Confirm Folder Delete message box is displayed, asking you to confirm that you want to delete the folder and its contents. If you select No, the deletion procedure is canceled. To continue,

Choose: Yes

The Personal folder and all the files within it are removed. The All Folders area now only displays the School Work folder and subfolders.

You are now ready to exit Explorer.

Restore the Exploring window to its original size and close the window.

Now you are ready to quit Windows 95.

Choose Shut Down from the Start menu.

If you are turning the computer off, wait until the screen message is displayed indicating that it is safe to shut off your computer.

WARNING!

To avoid damaging files, always shut down Windows before you turn off your computer.

LAB REVIEW

■ ■ ■ ■ ■ ■ ■ ■ ■ ■ ■

Key Terms

active area   WN86
All Folders area   WN82
associated file   WN67
cascade   WN77
Clipboard   WN85
Contents area   WN82
copy   WN85
current folder   WN93
cut   WN85
description bar   WN82
destination   WN85
drag and drop   WN95
Explorer   WN81
extend a selection   WN98
file   WN65
filename   WN92
filename extension   WN92
folder   WN65
hierarchy   WN83
main folder   WN83
move   WN97
paste   WN85
source   WN85
subfolder   WN65
tile   WN77
toolbar   WN68
Tooltip   WN69
tree   WN83

Command Summary

Command	Shortcut Key	Button	Action
File/Se**n**d to			Copies selected folder and/or files directly to a disk
File/New/**F**older			Creates a new folder
File/Rena**m**e			Changes name of a folder or file
File/P**r**operties		⬜	Displays properties associated with selected object
File/**C**lose		⬜	Closes active window
Edit/Cu**t**	Ctrl + X	⬜	Removes selected object and copies it to the Clipboard
Edit/**C**opy	Ctrl + C	⬜	Copies selected object to the Clipboard
Edit/**P**aste	Ctrl + V	⬜	Pastes selected object to new location
Edit/Select **A**ll	Ctrl + A		Selects all folders and/or files in active window
View/**T**oolbar			Turns on/off display of toolbar
View/Lar**g**e Icons		⬜	Displays folders and files as large icons
View/S**m**all Icons		⬜	Displays folders and files as small icons
View/**L**ist		⬜	Displays folders and files as a list
View/**D**etails		⬜	Displays all folder and file details
View/Arrange **I**cons/by **N**ame		Name	Organizes icons alphabetically by name
View/Arrange **I**cons/by **T**ype		Type	Organizes icons by type of files
View/Arrange **I**cons/by Si**z**e		Size	Organizes icons by size of files
View/Arrange **I**cons/by **D**ate		Modified	Organizes icons by last modification date of files

Matching

1. Match the following with the correct definition or function.

1) Contents area	_____	a. file type that is associated with an application
2) source	_____	b. changes name of a folder or file
3)	_____	c. temporary storage area
4) Clipboard	_____	d. displays folders and files as large icons
5)	_____	e. the location you copy or move from
6) associated file	_____	f. represents a folder
7) Rename	_____	g. displays folders and files as a list
8)	_____	h. represents a Help file
9)	_____	i. contains files that are related
10) folder	_____	j. area of Exploring window that displays folders and files in selected disks or folders

2. Use the figure below to match each action with its result.

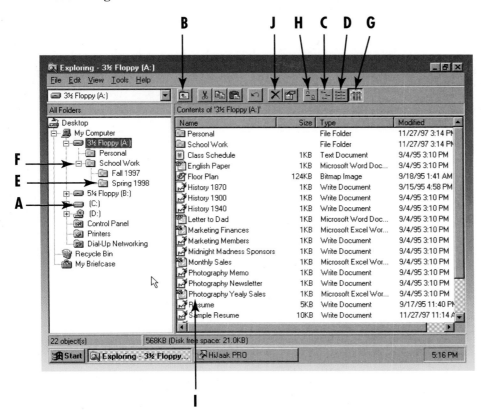

Action	Result
1) click F	_____ **a.** opens the Spring 1998 folder
2) click B	_____ **b.** displays files as small icons
3) click G	_____ **c.** displays file details
4) double-click A	_____ **d.** hides folders
5) click E	_____ **e.** selects a file
6) click I	_____ **f.** displays files as a list
7) click D	_____ **g.** expands the drive icon
8) click H	_____ **h.** displays files as large icons
9) click C	_____ **i.** moves up one level
10) click J	_____ **j.** deletes selection

3. In the following Windows 95 Exploring window, several items are identified by letters. Enter the correct term for each item in the space provided.

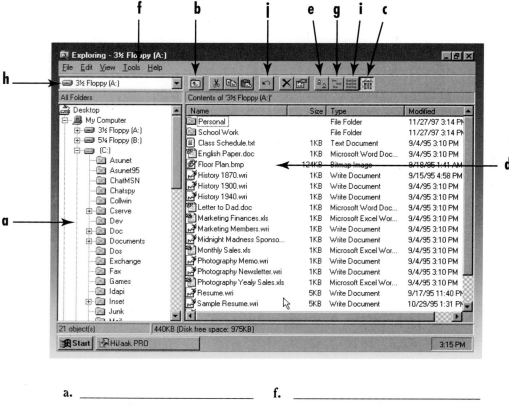

a. _____   f. _____

b. _____   g. _____

c. _____   h. _____

d. _____   i. _____

e. _____   j. _____

Fill-In Questions

1. Complete the following statements by filling in the blanks with the correct terms.

a. Storing related files in _____ keeps the disk organized and makes it much easier to locate files.

b. A _____ is used to identify the contents of a file.

c. A(n) _____ is a file that has a specific application program attached to it.

d. The _____ command layers open windows, displaying the active window fully and only the title bars of any other open windows behind it.

e. _____ is an application that helps you view and organize the files on your disk.

f. All Windows applications include features that allow you to _____, _____, and _____ selections.

g. A mouse shortcut for moving and copying files is to _____ a file.

h. To cancel the last action or command, use the _____ command.

i. To select several files at the same time, hold down _____ while clicking the file icons.

j. A _____ or tree is a graphic representation of the organization on a disk.

HANDS-ON PRACTICE EXERCISES

Step by Step

Rating System   ☆ Easy
☆☆ Moderate
☆☆☆ Difficult

☆
1. The Windows 95 program includes a Tour of Windows 95 that introduces and explains many of the basic Windows features. This problem will use the Tour of Windows 95 to reinforce many of the features presented in this lab.

> You need the Windows 95 CD or the Tour must be loaded on your system before you can complete this problem. Your instructor will provide you with instructions for loading the Tour of Windows 95.

a. Load the Tour of Windows 95.

b. Choose Exploring Your Disk from the Welcome to Windows 95 Tour menu. As you read and work through the tour, answer the following questions:

1) How do you find out what's inside something?

2) What does the hard disk contain?

3) Before you can work with a file, what must you do?

4) How do you close a menu?

c. Next choose Finding a File from the Welcome to Windows 95 Tour menu. As you read and work through the tour, answer the following questions:

1) What command could you use to locate a file?

2) What do you type in the Named text box?

3) What is the New Search option button used for?

    4) How did you find the Letter to Robert file?

   d.   Exit the Tour of Windows 95.

2. You are working on a project for your computer class that requires you to create multiple documents on a subject of your choice using several different applications. You have created your documents on the topic of photography. After creating several documents and storing them on your disk in the main folder, you have decided to organize the documents into folders to make them easier to locate.

   a.   Create a new folder named Computer Project on your data disk to store your files for this project.

   b.   Create subfolders for the different sections of the project, including folders for word processing documents, graphics, and financial documents.

   c.   Move the files Photography Memo and Photography Newsletter to the word processing folder.

   d.   Move the file Monthly Sales to the graphics folder.

   e.   Copy the file Photography Yearly Sales to the financial folder.

   f.   Confirm that all the files have been moved or copied to the correct folders.

3. You have been elected to the position of Recording Secretary for the Marketing Association club at your school. The association keeps records on finances, members, and sponsors. You would like to set up a disk to keep track of the files you create for the association.

   a.   Using Windows Explorer, create two new folders on your data disk. Name one Finances, and name the other People. Under the People folder create two subfolders, one for Members and the other for Sponsors.

   b.   Make the main folder active.

   c.   Move the file Marketing Finances to the Finance folder.

   d.   Copy the Marketing Members file to the Members subfolder.

   e.   Delete the Marketing Members file from the main folder.

   f.   Copy the three sponsor files from the main folder to the Sponsors subfolder.

   g.   Confirm that all the files have been copied or moved to the folders.

   h.   Close the Exploring window.

4. In this lab you used many, but not all, of the taskbar features. In this problem you will learn about other features of the taskbar. Use the taskbar and answer the following questions.

a.   Double-click on the time in the taskbar. What happened?

b.   Use What's This? Help for information on the Date/Time Properties dialog box. Describe the date and time properties that can be changed. Close the dialog box.

c.   Select Properties from the taskbar shortcut menu. Turn on the Auto Hide property. Choose OK. What happened to the taskbar?

d.   To redisplay the taskbar, move the mouse pointer to the bottom of the window. Then open the taskbar Properties dialog box and turn off the Auto Hide taskbar property.

e.   The taskbar can be moved along any border of the screen. Move it to each border and describe what happens to the desktop and the taskbar. Return the taskbar to the bottom of the window.

On Your Own

5. The Find command on the Start menu can be used to locate files on your system disk or data disk.

a.   Use Help to learn how to use this feature. Which search type do you think would take longest and why?

b.   Use Find to locate all the files on your hard disk (C) that contain the word "Window" in the name.

c.   Locate all files that were modified during the last month on your hard disk. How may files did you find?

d.   Locate all files containing the text "Sponsors" on your data disk. How many files did you find?

e.   Close Find.

6. You are the manager of 12 employees, all of whom are going to share files on a file server. Describe how you plan to allocate a private folder for each employee and how you plan to set up folders for the accounting, research, and cost management projects your employees will be working on.

Windows 95: Disk Organization

File and Folder Names

Both files and folders are assigned names that are used to identify contents of the file or folder.

Hierachy of Folders

The organization of folders, subfolders, and files on your disk is called a hierachy or tree.

Files and Folders

The information on your computer is stored as files. Folders contain files that are related.

Arranging Windows

Windows can be arranged on the desktop: cascaded, tiled horizontally, or tiled vertically.

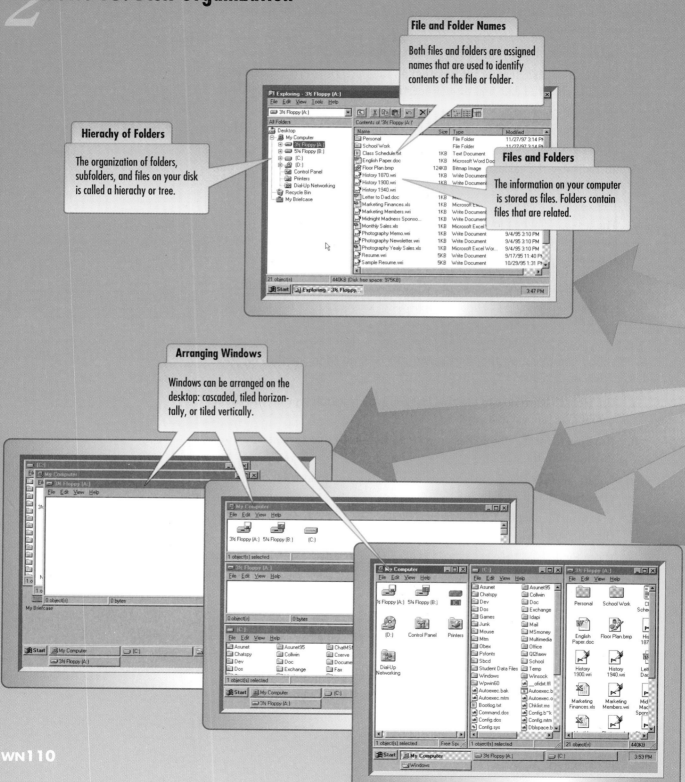

Undo

The Undo feature allows you to reverse your last action or command.

Toolbar

The toolbar contains buttons that are shortcuts for many of the most common menu commands.

Concepts

Files and Folders
File and Folder Names
Hierarchy of Folders

Arranging Windows

Toolbar
Undo

Cut, Copy, and Paste
Drag and Drop

Cut, Copy, and Paste

All Windows applications include features that allow you to remove (cut), duplicate (copy), and insert (paste) information from one location to another.

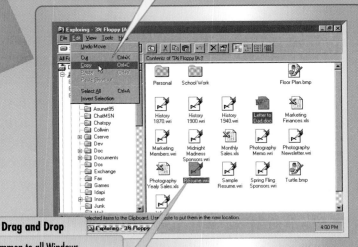

Drag and Drop

Common to all Windows applications is the ability to copy or move selections by dragging and dropping.

Using Windows 95 Applications

Not long ago, trained specialists were required to perform many day-to-day operations. Secretaries used typewriters to produce typed correspondence. Accountants used pens and paper ledgers to record and analyze data. Artists used pen and paper to produce graphic artwork. Now with the development of specialized applications software, you can easily do many of these jobs yourself.

There are applications software programs that help you create written correspondence, drawings and artwork, or financial statements and budgets. Others help you maintain records and produce informational reports. And still others help you connect and communicate with other computers.

In this lab you will learn to use two application software programs that are included with Windows 95: WordPad and Paint. Learning how to use these programs builds upon the skills you acquired while learning about the operating system. In addition, you will learn about features that are common to other applications that run under Windows 95. This will make it easier for you to learn to use new applications in the future.

Concept Overview

The following concepts will be introduced in this lab:

1. Word Processor	Word processing applications are designed to help you create, edit, and print documents.
2. Editing	The process of correcting or changing existing text is called editing.
3. Selecting Text	Selecting highlights the text that will be affected by your next action.
4. Font Size	Font size refers to the height of printed characters.
5. Saving Files	Saving creates a permanent copy of your onscreen document in a file on a disk.
6. Drawing Programs	Drawing programs are used to create illustrations.
7. Objects	An object is any set of information created in one application, then inserted or stored in a document that was created using a different application.
8. Linking and Embedding	When objects are copied from one application to another, they can be inserted into the receiving document as a pasted object, a linked object, or an embedded object.
9. Shortcut Icons	Shortcut icons provide quick access to the associated feature.

Part 1

Using WordPad

In addition to the programs that run as part of Windows 95, such as Windows Explorer, Windows 95 includes several small programs that are designed to help you with your work, or amuse you while passing time. Some, but not all, are installed automatically on the hard disk of the computer when Windows 95 is installed. Others must be added individually. The table below lists and briefly describes many of these programs.

> Refer to Help for information on adding programs.

Application	Description
Briefcase	Quickly transfers files between a laptop and desktop computer
CD Player	Plays music from CDs using the CD disk drive
Calculator	Performs calculations
Character Map	Inserts symbols/characters in documents
Clipboard Viewer	Displays contents of Windows Clipboard
Desktop Wallpaper	Background images for desktop
Document Templates	Creates new document for most common programs
DriveSpace	Disk compression program
Games	Solitaire, Minesweeper, Hearts, and Free Cell
(continued)	

OPERATING SYSTEM

Application	Description
HyperTerminal	Connects via modem to a remote computer, sends/receives files
Microsoft Network	Standard on-line service offering electronic mail, bulletin boards, newsgroups, etc.
Microsoft Exchange	Electronic mailbox
Media Player	Plays audio, video, and animation files
Mouse Pointers	Variety of easy-to-see pointers
Net Watcher	Monitors network server and connections
Online User's Guide	Online version of user guide
Paint	Used to create, modify, or view pictures
Phone Dialer	Dials phone numbers in your personal phone book
Quick View	Previews document without opening it
ScanDisk	Checks disks for errors
Screen Savers	Displays moving images when computer is idle
Sound Recorder	Records and plays sounds
System Monitor	Monitors system performance
System Resource Meter	Views system resource levels
Window 95 Tour	Teaches a few basics on Windows 95
WordPad	Word processor for short memos and documents

Many of these additional programs are in the Accessories section of the Programs menu. To display the accessories on your system,

Choose: Start/Programs/Accessories

All the accessory programs that are available on your system are displayed. One of the most useful programs is WordPad, a word processing program designed to produce day-to-day business and personal documents.

Concept 1: Word Processor

Word processing applications are designed to help you create, edit, and print documents. **Documents** are any kind of text material such as memos, letters, and research papers. Word processors have replaced the typewriter, and moreover have greatly enhanced what a typewriter could do. The biggest advantage of a word processor is that it displays the text as you type it on your computer screen rather than on paper. This makes it easy to make changes and corrections onscreen before the document is printed on paper. Word processors are probably the most used of all software programs and are credited with producing the highest gains in user productivity.

You are planning a party to celebrate a friend's 21st birthday. You decide to use WordPad to create and print an invitation. The completed invitation will look like that shown in Figure 3-1 below.

Figure 3-1

To open WordPad,

Click: 📝 **WordPad**

If necessary, maximize the window.

Your screen should be similar to Figure 3-2 shown in the box on the next page.

The WordPad application is opened in its own window, and the taskbar displays a button for the open application. The parts of the WordPad window are described on the next page.

Parts of the WordPad Window

Figure 3-2

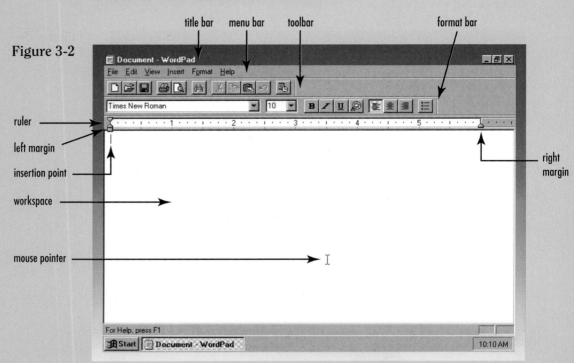

The title bar displays the temporary filename, Document, followed by the name of the program. The temporary filename is displayed until you save the file and give it a more descriptive name. Below the title bar is a menu bar displaying six menus: File, Edit, View, Insert, Format, and Help. The toolbar contains button shortcuts for many of the most frequently used menu commands. Displayed below the toolbar is the **format bar**. The format bar contains buttons representing the most frequently used text-editing and text-layout features.

The **ruler** is displayed below the format bar. The ruler shows the line length in inches. The zero position on the ruler marks the location of the left margin. The ◣ symbol on the right end of the ruler at the 6-inch position marks the right margin. The ruler is used to set tab stops and indents for selected paragraphs. The ruler can also be used to change the page margins and to help place items on the page.

The large blank area below the ruler is the **workspace**. This is where your work is displayed. The insertion point is positioned in the upper left corner of the workspace, ready for you to begin typing. When the mouse pointer is positioned in the workspace, it appears as an I-beam, just as it does in a text box of a dialog box.

If any of the WordPad window features are not displayed, use the View menu to select the appropriate option to turn on the feature.

You would like to enter the text for the invitation next. To enter text in WordPad, simply begin typing. As you are typing, the insertion point moves to show you where the next character will appear. The character after the insertion point is the **active character**. This is the character that will be affected by your next action.

While typing, you will certainly make typing errors or you will want to change what you have typed. The process of correcting or changing existing text is called **editing**.

Concept 2: Editing

A word processor excels in its ability to change or edit a document. You can quickly delete a character, word, sentence, or paragraph and replace it with new text. There are many methods you can use to edit text. The two most common are to use the ⟨←Backspace⟩ key to delete unwanted characters to the left of the insertion point, or the ⟨Delete⟩ key to remove the active character. Then you can retype the text correctly.

The directional keys or the mouse are used to move the insertion point back within the text. To move the insertion point with the mouse, position the I-beam at the location in the text where you want the insertion point to be and click the left mouse button.

Make sure the pointer is an I-beam before clicking to move the insertion point.

To begin the invitation,

Type: Party, Party, Party -- Get Ready to Party!
Press: ⟨←Enter⟩

Pressing ⟨←Enter⟩ ends a line and moves the insertion point to the beginning of the next line. To create a blank line,

Press: ⟨←Enter⟩

When the insertion point is at the beginning of a line and ⟨←Enter⟩ is pressed, a blank line is created.

To continue the invitation, enter the following text without pressing the ⟨←Enter⟩ key,

Type: We're having a pool party and barbecue to celebrate Dan's 21st birthday! Bring your suit and a smile, we will provide the rest.

Notice that as you type, the text automatically moves to the next line when it reaches the right margin defined by the 6-inch mark on the ruler. This feature of word processors is called **word wrap**.

Press: ⟨←Enter⟩ (2 times)

To continue the invitation, type the text shown below. Press ←Enter at the end of each line and follow each colon with two spaces.

When: Friday August 7
Time: 7:00 p.m.
Where: [Your Name]

Press: ←Enter

Your screen should be similar to Figure 3-3.

Figure 3-3

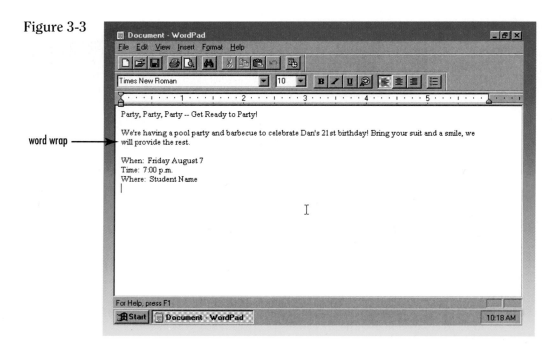

word wrap

Check your typing for any errors. If you see any errors, correct them using the editing features discussed in Concept 2: Editing.

Centering Text

After entering the text of the invitation, you would like to improve its appearance by centering all the lines of the invitation between the margins and increasing the type size of the characters. Enhancing the appearance of a document is called **formatting**.

Before you can apply the formatting effects, you first need to select the text you want to format.

Concept 3: Selecting Text

Selecting text highlights the text that will be affected by your next action, much like selecting files or folders before copying or moving. There are many methods you can use to select an area of text.

The most common method is to drag the mouse to select an area of text, just as in a text box. You can drag in any direction in the document to extend the highlight. You can drag diagonally across text to extend the highlight from the character the insertion point is on to the last character in the selection. You can also drag in the opposite direction to deselect text. The keyboard can be used to select text by holding down ⇧Shift while pressing a directional key. Either method requires that you move the insertion point to the beginning or end of the area to be selected before you select it. You can also select the entire document using the Select All command on the Edit menu in all Windows 95 applications.

A selection is cleared by clicking anywhere outside the selection or by pressing a direction key.

To select the entire document,

Choose: <u>E</u>dit/Select A<u>ll</u>

The keyboard shortcut is Ctrl + A.

All the text in the invitation is highlighted, indicating it is selected.

The format bar buttons are used to format text in the document. The ☰, ☰, and ☰ buttons are used to align text with the left margin, center it between the margins, and align it with the right margin. To center the text,

Click: ☰ Center

The menu equivalent is F<u>o</u>rmat/ <u>P</u>aragraph/<u>A</u>lignment/Center.

Your screen should be similar to Figure 3-4.

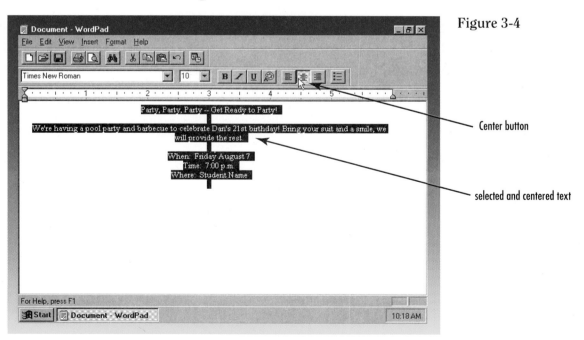

Figure 3-4

Center button

selected and centered text

The selected lines of text are centered between the margins.

Changing Type Size

To further enhance the appearance of the invitation, you would like to increase the font size of the currently selected text.

> **Concept 4: Font Size**
>
> **Font size**, also commonly called type size or point size, refers to the height and width of printed characters. Font size is measured in **points**, which refers to the height of the character, with each point about $1/72$ inch. Most documents use a type size of 10 or 12 points. The larger the number of points, the larger the size of the characters.

The menu equivalent to size text is Format/Font/Size.

The Font Size drop-down list button in the format bar is used to change font size. The text box shows the font size of characters in the selection. If the selection included mixed font sizes, the text box would be blank. Because the font size is the same for all characters in this selection, it displays 10. To change the size, you can type the new font size in the text box and press ←Enter . Alternatively, you can select from a list of font sizes that is displayed when you open the drop-down list. You will increase the size to 16 points by selecting the size from the drop-down list. To do this,

Click ▼ to display the drop-down list.

Click: 10 ▼   Font Size

The drop-down list of font size options is displayed.

Select: 16

Click outside the selection to clear it.

Clear the highlight and, if necessary, move to the top of the document.

Your screen should be similar to Figure 3-5.

Font Size button

Figure 3-5

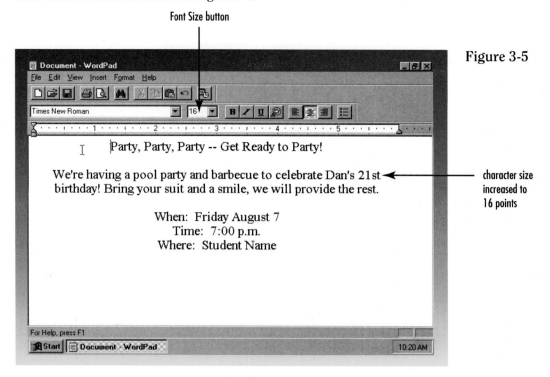

character size
increased to
16 points

The text appears on the screen in 16-point font size, as it will appear when printed.

Next you would like to make the invitation title line an even larger font size than the rest of the text.

Using either selection method presented in Concept 3: Selecting Text, select the invitation title only.

The entire line is selected.

Increase the title to 24 points.

Adding Color to Text

While the title is still selected, you would also like to apply a color to the title text. The Color button on the format bar can be used to change the color of the text.

Click: Color

The menu equivalent is F*o*rmat/*F*ont/*C*olor.

A drop-down list of 16 colors is displayed.

To select a color, click on a color of your choice. Then clear the highlight.

Your screen should be similar to Figure 3-6.

Figure 3-6

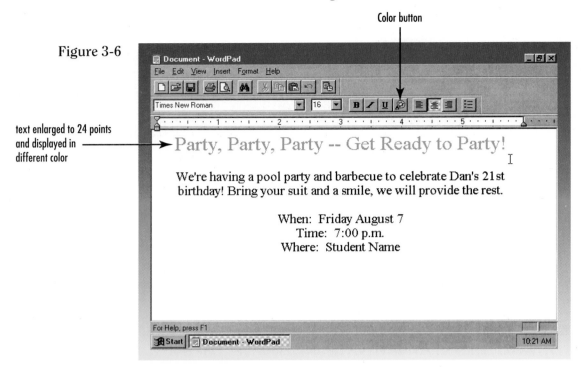

text enlarged to 24 points and displayed in different color

Color button

Saving a File

Now that the text of the invitation is how you want it to appear, you will save your work to a file. If you do not save your work, the document will no longer exist when you exit WordPad.

Concept 5: Saving Files

While working on a document, your changes are stored temporarily in the computer's memory. Not until you **save** the document as a file on a disk are you safe from losing your work due to a power failure or other mishap.

Two commands found on the File menu of all Windows programs can be used to save a file: Save and Save As. The Save command saves a document using the same path and filename as the existing disk file, by replacing the contents of the file with the changes you have made. The Save As command allows you to select a different path and/or provide a different filename. This command lets you save both an original version of a document and a revised document as two separate files.

When you save a file for the first time, either command can be used. Although many programs create automatic backup files if your work is accidentally interrupted, it is still a good idea to save your work frequently.

The Save button on the toolbar can be used to save a file.

Click:　　　 Save

> The menu and keyboard equivalents are File/Save and Ctrl + S.

Your screen should be similar to Figure 3-7.

Save As dialog box　　Save In drop-down list box

Figure 3-7

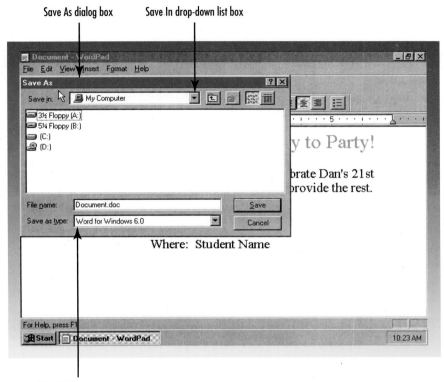

> Your dialog box may display different folders or files.

default file association

Whenever you save a file for the first time, the Save As dialog box is displayed so you can specify where you want the file saved and the filename. You want to save the file to your data disk.

Open the Save In drop-down list box.

Select:　　A: (or the drive containing your data disk)

The selected location is displayed in the Save In text box.

The Save As Type drop-down list box displays the name of the application that will be associated with the saved file. If you do not specify a file extension when naming a file, the extension associated with the selected application will automatically be added to the filename. You can also select a different application from the drop-down list box to change the association, or include a specific file extension when naming the file to override the selection. In Figure 3-7 the default associates the file with the Word for Windows 6.0 application.

You are now ready to name the file.

Select the existing default filename, Document.doc, in the File Name text box.

> Refer to Lab 2 for information about associated files and file naming rules.

> Your computer may associate the file with another word processor or with WordPad.

> Drag or double-click on the word to select it.

As soon as you begin typing, the existing filename will be erased. You will name the file Invitation and include the WordPad file extension, .wri. To name the file,

> The filename can be entered in either uppercase or lowercase letters.

Type: Invitation.wri
Choose: <u>S</u>ave

The document is saved to the disk using the specified filename. The new filename now appears in the title bar and in the taskbar button.

Next you want to add a picture of balloons to the invitation using the Paint application program, which is also included with Windows 95. Because you will use WordPad again shortly, you will not exit the application before opening Paint.

Minimize the WordPad window.

Using Paint

The Paint application is a drawing program that is used to create graphic images.

Concept 6: Drawing Programs

Drawing programs are used to create illustrations. They allow you to create attractive, sophisticated line art by combining lines, arcs, circles, and other shapes. These programs are commonly used by professional illustrators to produce artwork used in publications such as books and magazines.

When you opened the WordPad application, you used the Programs command in the Start menu. Another way to open a program and create a new document is to use the desktop shortcut menu.

> Right-click the desktop background.

Display the desktop shortcut menu.

The New command is used to create new documents.

Select: <u>N</u>ew

Next you need to specify the type of file you want to create. The Paint program creates graphics that consist of many small dots on the screen called a **bitmap**. These files are saved as bitmap files.

> Bitmap files have a file extension of .bmp.

Choose: Bitmap Image

Your screen should be similar to Figure 3-8.

Figure 3-8

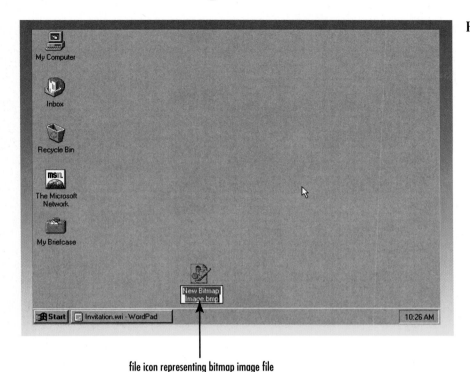

file icon representing bitmap image file

A file icon representing an application that is associated with bitmap images is displayed on the desktop. The text under the icon displays the default button name "New Bitmap Image.bmp." You will replace the default name with the filename you will use to name the balloon file, just as you did when naming a new folder. To do this,

Type: **Balloons.bmp**
Press: ⟵Enter

Then, to open the Balloons file and the associated application, Paint,

Double-click: Balloons.bmp

If necessary, maximize the Paint window so that more workspace is displayed to create the drawing.

Your screen should be similar to Figure 3-9 on the next page.

The Paint program is loaded with the Balloons file open. You now have two programs open and running as indicated by the two buttons in the taskbar. The parts of the Paint window are described below.

Parts of the Paint Window

Figure 3-9

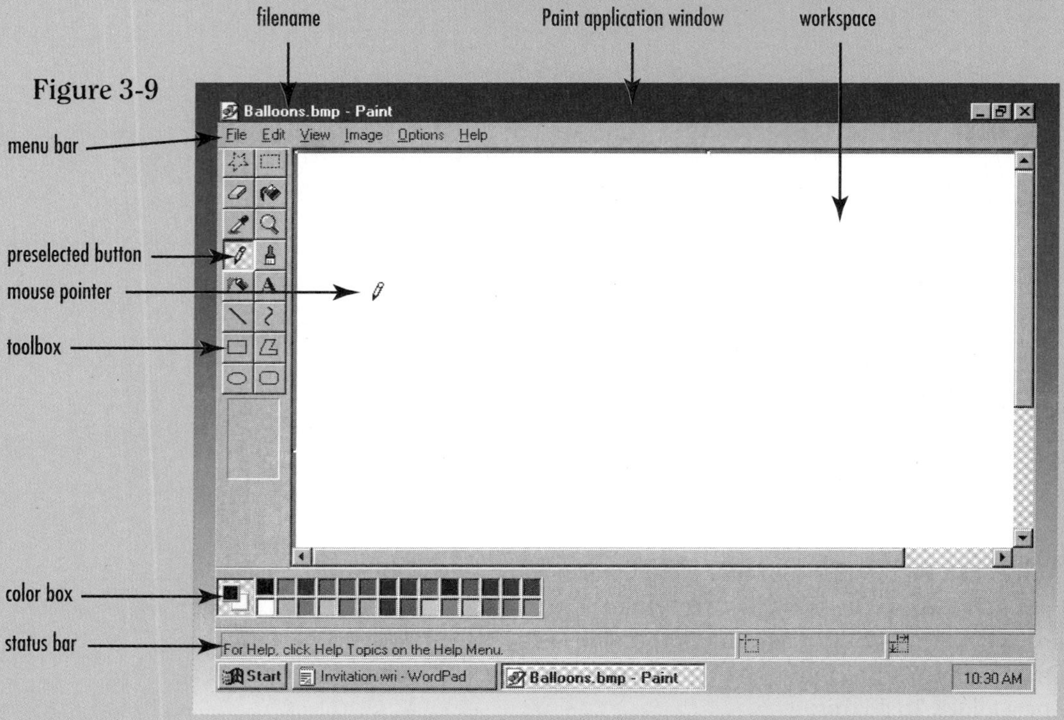

The Paint program has some of the same features as the WordPad program, including a workspace, a menu bar, and a toolbar, called a **toolbox** in Paint. By default the toolbox is displayed on the left edge of the window. Displayed at the bottom of the window is the color box and status bar.

If these features are not displayed, use the View menu to turn them on.

You would like to draw a picture of three balloons that you can copy into the invitation you created using WordPad. The toolbox buttons are used to draw shapes, fill shapes with colors, edit the drawing, and so on.

Read the Tooltip and the description in the status bar for each of the toolbox buttons to find out what they do.

The preselected button is the Pencil button. You can tell it is selected because it appears depressed. The mouse pointer appears as a ✎ when this button is selected, indicating that when it is used a free-form line will be created.

You can also use Help to learn more about the Paint program.

Creating Shapes

First you will draw a balloon in the center of the window. The button creates an ellipse or circular shape. To use this button to draw the balloon,

Click: Ellipse

Your screen should be similar to Figure 3-10.

selected fill style

selected button

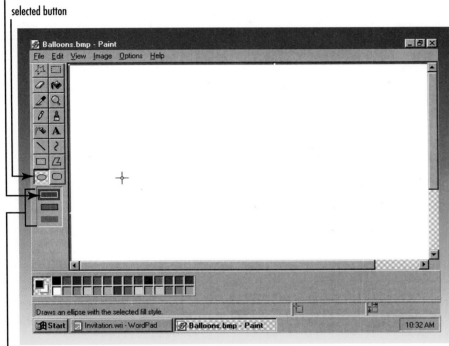

Figure 3-10

fill-style buttons

The button appears depressed in the toolbox, indicating it is selected. Whichever tool is selected will be drawn when you drag or click in the workspace. Notice that there are now three additional buttons, called fill-style buttons, displayed at the bottom of the toolbox. The first button will draw an ellipse with an outline border in the selected fill color without filling the object. The second button will draw an outline border and also fill the object with the selected fill color. The last fill style will create an object without a border using the selected fill color. The default style of a border with no fill is acceptable for this drawing.

> The selected fill style button appears highlighted.

When you move the mouse pointer into the workspace, it changes to a +. To begin drawing, move the mouse pointer to where you want the circle to begin.

Point to: top center of the workspace

A circle or ellipse is created by dragging the mouse until the shape is displayed on the screen as you want it to look. When the shape is how you want it to appear, release the mouse button.

> Drag the mouse to create a balloon of a shape and size of your choice.

Your screen should be similar to Figure 3-11.

> Dragging diagonally creates an ellipse. Hold ⇧Shift while dragging to create a perfect circle.

Figure 3-11

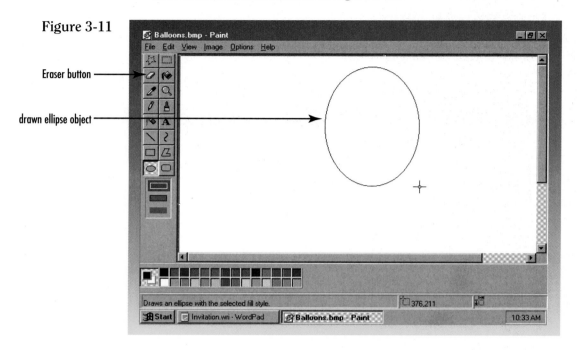

Eraser button

drawn ellipse object

The mouse pointer is still a ⌖, indicating it is ready to create another ellipse. Not until you select another tool button will the ellipse shape be turned off.

If you do not like the shape, you can use Edit/Undo to delete the shape and try again.

> In a similar manner, draw two more balloons, one on either side of the first (make one of them overlap another).

To clean up the drawing, you can use the Eraser button to delete the part of the outline on the overlapping balloon that is in the foreground. To do this,

> Undo can be used to undelete your last three actions in Paint. The Undo command shortcut is Ctrl + Z. There is no Undo button.

Click: 🗑 **Eraser**

The mouse pointer changes to a □, indicating that any line you drag it over will be erased.

> Drag the mouse over the line you want to erase. If you make a mistake, use Undo to restore the line and try again.

Next you would like to add bottoms (ties) to the balloons (see Figure 3-12 for reference as to how the ties should appear). Since there is no tool that will create this particular shape, you will use the ▱ Polygon tool to draw the shapes you need.

Click: ▱ **Polygon tool**

To use the ⬚ Polygon tool, point to the location where you want the shape to start and then drag and click on the corner locations. Double-click when the shape is complete. If the shape is not a closed shape, the program will close it for you by adding a final line.

Draw bottoms on all three balloons.

To complete the drawing, you would like to add strings at the bottoms of the balloons. You can use the ⬚ Line tool button to draw the strings.

Click: ⬚ **Line**

To use the ⬚ Line tool, point to where you want the line to start and drag to the location where you want the line to end. When you release the mouse button, the line is created.

Draw three lines from the balloons to a point below the balloons.

Your screen should be similar to Figure 3-12.

Line tool

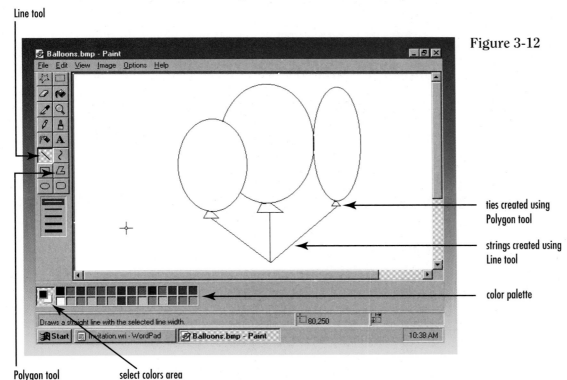

Figure 3-12

ties created using Polygon tool

strings created using Line tool

color palette

Polygon tool   select colors area

Adding Colors

Next you would like to add colors to the balloons. You do this by selecting colors from the color box. The color box consists of two areas: the select colors area and the color palette. The select colors area displays the currently selected foreground and background colors. The box in the foreground shows the currently selected foreground color, and the box in the background shows the background color. By default the foreground color is black while the background color is white.

The background color is selected by right-clicking on a color in the palette, and the foreground color is selected by left-clicking on a color. If you select colors before creating a shape, the shape's outline is created using the foreground color while the inside of the shape is filled with the background color. You can also fill an existing shape with color.

You would like to fill the balloons with different colors.

Select colors from the palette for the foreground and background.

You can fill a shape with a different color after it is created using the 🐾 Fill with Color tool.

Click: 🐾 **Fill with Color**

The mouse pointer changes to a 🐾, indicating it can be used to fill an object. To use the 🐾 tool, point to the area you want to fill and click the left mouse button to fill the shape with the foreground color, or click the right mouse button to fill the shape with the background color.

Fill a balloon with one of the colors you selected.

If the shape being filled has any breaks in its border, the filling color leaks through to the rest of the drawing area.

If the color leaks to another balloon or area, Undo the fill and fix the edge of the balloon using the ＼ Line tool. Then fill the shape again.

Next you will fill the tie. If you drew small ties, they may be difficult to fill. Carefully place the end of the paint stream inside the object before clicking the mouse button.

Fill the balloon tie with the same color.

Your screen should be similar to Figure 3-13.

> If the color appears in the wrong space, use Undo and try again.

Figure 3-13

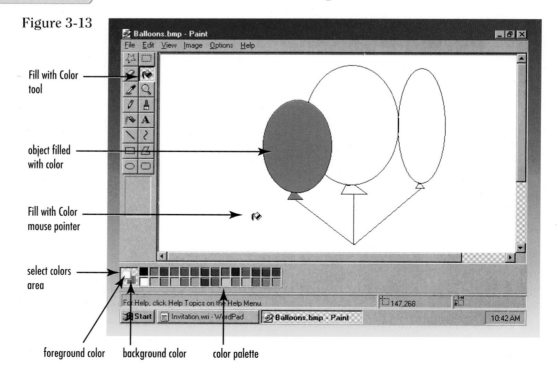

Fill with Color tool

object filled with color

Fill with Color mouse pointer

select colors area

foreground color   background color   color palette

In a similar manner, fill the other two balloons and their ties with color.

Now that you have completed the drawing, you are ready to paste a copy of it into the invitation. First you will save the changes you have made to the Balloon file.

Choose: **File/Save**

The Save command saves the document as it appears onscreen to the same filename, automatically replacing the original contents with the new contents.

Note: If you are ending your lab session now, close both the applications. Move the file icon Balloons.bmp to your data disk and quit Windows 95. When you begin Part 2, start WordPad and use File/Open to open the Invitation.wri document. Then start Paint and open the Balloons.bmp file. Copy Balloons.bmp from your data disk to the desktop.

Part 2

Copying the Graphic

To insert the picture of the balloons into the invitation, you will make a copy of the graphic and store it in the Clipboard. You can copy the entire workspace or any part of the screen by selecting an area. Since the drawing is much smaller than the entire screen, you will select just the drawing.

To select the drawing, you can use the 🔲 Free-Form Select or 🔲 Select tool. The 🔲 Free-Form Select tool allows you to draw an irregular shape around the part of the object you want to select, while the 🔲 Select tool allows you to select a rectangular area.

Click: 🔲 **Select**

The mouse pointer changes to a ✛. To use the selection tool, you drag the mouse to create a box around the area you want to copy. This is similar to selecting multiple files by creating a box around the file icons.

If necessary, first scroll the workspace to position the drawing in the workspace so it is entirely visible.

Click above the top-left corner of the drawing and drag the mouse pointer to the opposite corner to select the entire picture. If the box does not enclose the entire drawing, click anywhere outside the selection to clear the box and try again.

Your screen should be similar to Figure 3-14.

Select tool   selected object

Figure 3-14

Free-form
select tool

Then, to copy the selection to the Clipboard,

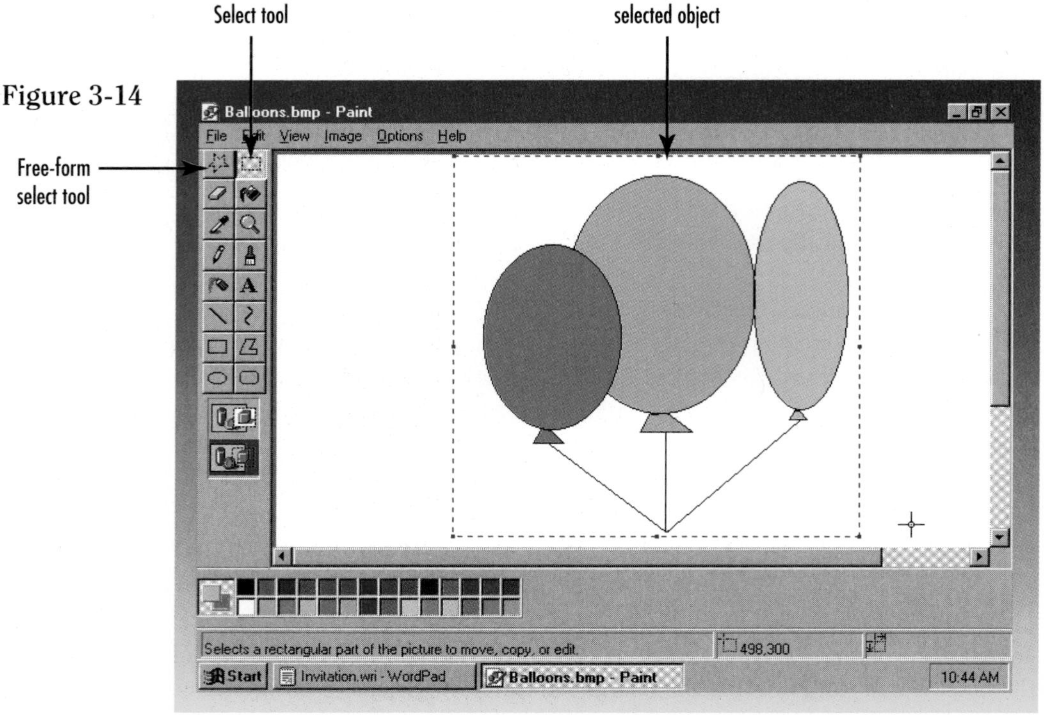

> The keyboard shortcut equivalent is Ctrl + C. Copy is also an option on the shortcut menu.

Choose: Edit/Copy

The contents of the selected area are copied to the Clipboard.

Viewing Clipboard Contents

You can view the contents of the Clipboard to verify that the selected graphic is stored in it using the Clipboard Viewer program. Clipboard Viewer is another application that is in the Accessories menu. To open the Clipboard Viewer,

> The Clipboard Viewer needs to be installed separately. See your instructor or skip this section if this option is not available.

Choose: Start/Programs/Accessories/Clipboard Viewer

Your screen should be similar to Figure 3-15.

Clipboard Viewer displays copy of
image that is stored in Clipboard

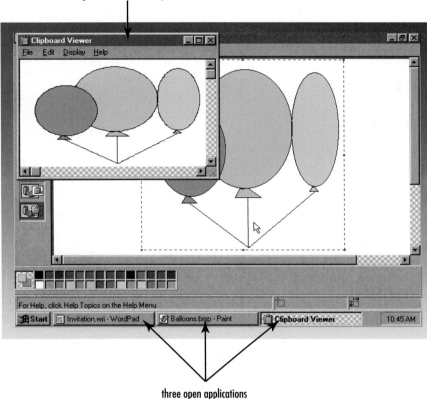

Figure 3-15

three open applications

The Clipboard Viewer is opened and displays a copy of the balloons graphic. The Viewer is displayed in a window on top of the Paint program window; it has some of the same features as other applications, including a title bar and a menu bar. You now have three applications running at the same time as you can see from the taskbar.

You can leave the Clipboard Viewer open or close it. Since you opened the Viewer only to verify its contents, to close the application,

Click: Close

> The command equivalent is File/Exit.

Copying to Another Application

You are now ready to paste the picture into the WordPad document. To redisplay the WordPad window,

Click: 📄 invitation.wri - WordPad (on the taskbar)

You would like to paste the picture that is stored in the Clipboard into the top left corner of the invitation.

If necessary, move the insertion point to the top of the document.

To insert two blank lines above the text in the invitation and move to it,

Press: [←Enter] **2 times**
Press: [↑] **2 times**

The insertion point appears at the center of the blank line because the Center feature was in effect for the line the insertion point was on when the two new lines were created. To return the alignment to left,

Click: [≡] **Left**

The insertion point is positioned on the left margin. The information that is stored in Clipboard is an object that you want to copy to another application.

Concept 7: Objects

An **object** is any set of information created using a Windows application, and that is inserted and stored in a document created using a different application. The object can be text, graphics, or any other element created in the source application, called the **server**. The file containing the original object is the **source file**. The file receiving the copy of the object is the **destination document**. This document is also commonly referred to as a **compound document** because it is made up of objects from multiple applications.

An object can be copied from one application to another as a pasted object, an embedded object, or a linked object.

Concept 8: Linking and Embedding

Pasting an object simply places an image of the object in the compound document. If possible, the object is converted into a format that the destination document can edit. If this is not possible, the image cannot be updated or edited.

An object that is **linked** also displays only a graphic representation of the object; however, it also stores the location of the object's source file, creating a connection between the source and the destination document. Any changes made to the object in the source file are automatically made to the image in the destination document.

When an object is **embedded**, it is stored in the compound document. Because the entire object, along with a reference to the source application, is included in the compound document, it can be edited from within the compound document by opening the server application it references if it is loaded on the computer you are using. Any editing changes are made to the embedded object only, while the original source file is not changed.

DDE (Dynamic Data Exchange) and **OLE** (Object Linking and Embedding) are the processes that allow the linking and embedding of information between applications. DDE creates linked objects and OLE creates embedded objects. Not all applications support object linking and embedding.

The Paste and Paste Special commands are used to insert a copy from the Clipboard into a document. Generally, the Paste command or 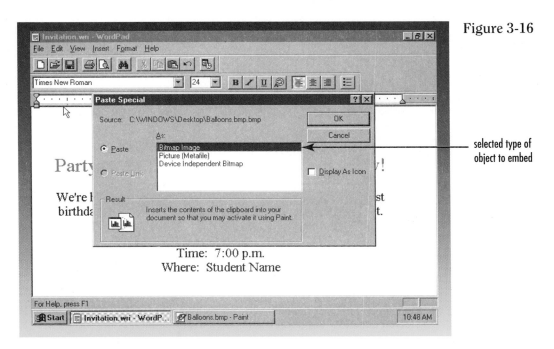 button simply inserts a copy of the Clipboard contents into a document without linking or embedding it. The Paste Special command allows you to create a link or to embed the Clipboard contents. To embed the Balloons object,

Choose: Edit/Paste Special

Your screen should be similar to Figure 3-16.

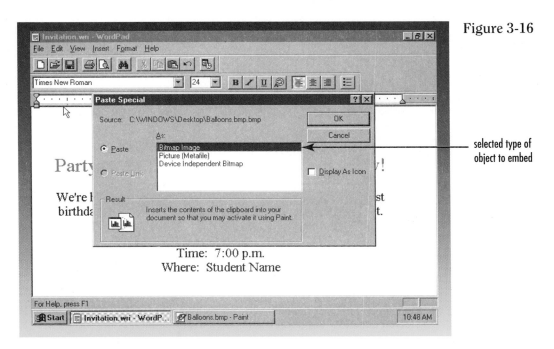

Figure 3-16

The Paste Special dialog box is displayed. The Paste option creates an embedded object. If necessary,

Select: Paste

The As list box lists three object types that can be selected. The type controls how the object will be inserted into the document. Because the object was created as a bitmap, this is the default selected type. In addition, the result area indicates that selecting this option will let you edit the image using Paint. If necessary,

Select: Bitmap Image
Choose: OK

Your screen should be similar to Figure 3-17.

Pasted object

Figure 3-17

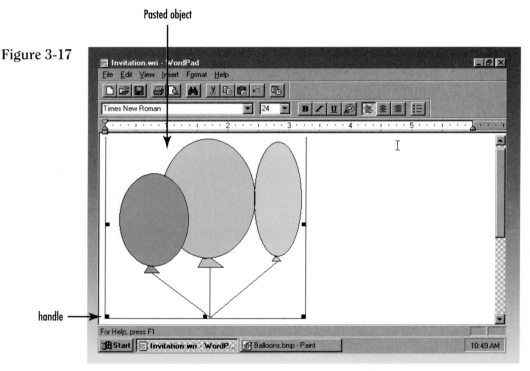

handle

The graphic of balloons that was stored in the Clipboard is pasted into the document. It is surrounded by a box and eight solid squares called **handles**. These indicate the object is selected and can be manipulated. You can adjust the size of any selected object by dragging the handles in the same manner as sizing windows.

Point to the handle in the lower right corner and drag the box outline until it is approximately a 1.5-inch square.

Deselect the graphic by clicking outside the image.

> Use the ruler as a guide for sizing the object.

Your screen should be similar to Figure 3-18.

sized object

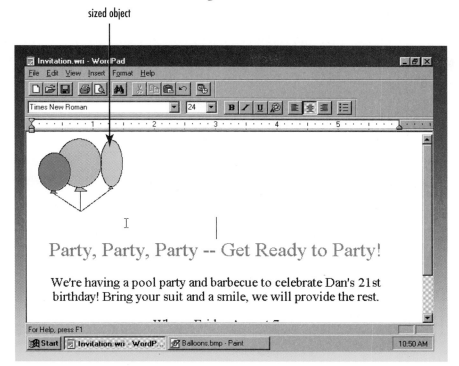

Figure 3-18

Next you want to copy another picture of the balloons into the invitation. To quickly move to the bottom of the document,

Press: Page Down

The insertion point is positioned at the end of the document. To make room for the second graphic, you need to insert a blank line.

Press: ←Enter

The insertion point should be displayed in the center of the line. You want the graphic centered, so there is no need to change the alignment.

If it is not centered, click 🔲.

The copy of the balloons graphic is still in the Clipboard. Anything you select and copy is stored in Clipboard until it is replaced by another copied item or you quit Windows. To insert the same picture,

Choose: Edit/Paste Special/OK

A second graphic of the balloons is added to the invitation.

Editing an Embedded Object

After looking at the inserted graphic, you decide you want to add some text inside the balloons. To edit an embedded object, you open the object server. This allows you to edit the embedded graphic from within WordPad.

> The menu equivalent is Edit/Bitmap Image Object/Edit.

Double-click: the bottom graphic

Your screen should be similar to Figure 3-19.

Figure 3-19

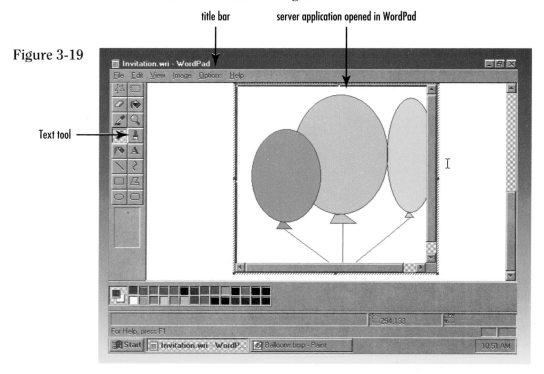

Paint (the server application) is opened within WordPad and the graphic appears in its own editing window. Notice that there is still only one Paint application button in the taskbar. This indicates that the Paint program has not been opened a second time in its own application window. Also notice that the title bar still displays "WordPad," and if you scroll up, the text of the invitation is still displayed. You now have access to the Paint menus and toolbar so you can edit the object while you are still in the WordPad document.

The Text tool ▣ is used to add text to a paint object. To add text to a balloon,

Click: ▣ Text

The mouse pointer changes to a ╋ when in the server editing window. When adding text, you first create a box, called a **text box**, then type the text inside it.

Drag to create a box inside the leftmost balloon.

The text box displays an insertion point and the Fonts dialog box is displayed. It shows the default type style and size that will be used when you type the text entry. These settings are acceptable.

Before typing the text, you can choose a color for the text. The color that will be applied to the text is the foreground color.

Select the foreground color of your choice.
To enter text in the balloon,

Type: Happy

To close the text box,

Click: **anywhere outside the box within the server editing window**

Create another text box in the middle balloon, select a text color, and enter the text "21st." In the third balloon, display the word "Dan." Deselect the text box.
Your screen should be similar to Figure 3-20.

> Click on the color button with the left mouse button to select a foreground color.

> You may need to adjust the size of the text box to accommodate the text.

Figure 3-20

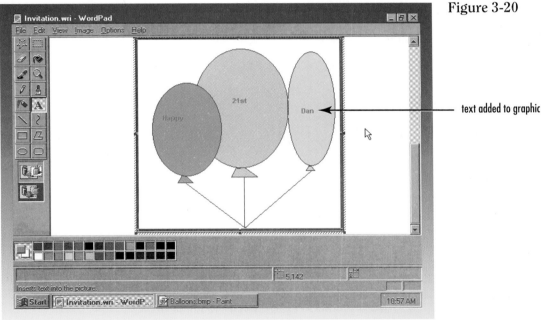

text added to graphic

To close the Paint program that is opened within WordPad, click anywhere outside the object.
To verify that the original picture file in Paint has not changed, switch to the Paint application window.
The text does not appear in the balloons.
Exit the Paint application.

Since no changes were made to the file, you are not prompted to save the file before the program is closed.

WordPad is displayed again, because it was the last used application.

Select the bottom graphic object and make it slightly larger.

> A single click selects the object.

Previewing and Printing the Document

To see how the invitation will look when it is printed, you can preview the document.

> The menu equivalent is File/Print Preview.

Click: 🖅 **Print Preview**

Your screen should be similar to Figure 3-21.

Figure 3-21

Preview window

Preview toolbar

margin

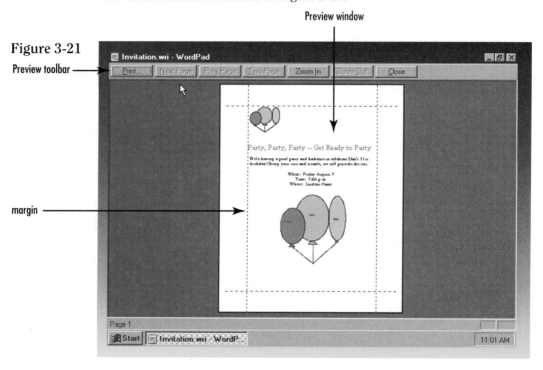

Preview displays the full page as it will appear when printed. The dotted lines indicate the margin areas. The Preview window has its own set of toolbar buttons. Some are dimmed because they are not available.

You like how the invitation looks and want to print the document.

> If you want to adjust the pictures on the invitation, choose Close. Then when you are done, select the Print Preview command again.

> Please consult your instructor for printing procedures that may differ from the directions provided.

Click: Print...

> You can also print using File/Print or 🖨 without previewing the document.

The Print dialog box is displayed. The active printer name is displayed at the top of the dialog box. The Print Range area of the dialog box lets you specify how much of the document you want printed. All is the default setting. You can also select to print individual pages or text that is selected in a document. The Copies area lets you specify the number of copies.

Now you are ready to instruct WordPad to print the document.

First turn on the printer and make any necessary adjustment to prepare the printer to print.

To print,

Choose: OK

If you need to select a different printer, your instructor will provide the printer to select.

The printer indicator icon 🖨 is displayed in the notification area of the taskbar while printing is in progress. If you double-click on the indicator, the Printer dialog box is displayed so you can see the printer status and settings and cancel a print job if needed.

The type of printer you use will determine how the balloons will be printed. Most black-and-white printers will print the balloons in shades of gray.

Now that the invitation is complete, you are ready to close the WordPad program.

Before closing the window, restore it to its original size. Close WordPad.

Because you modified the document since last saving it, you are prompted to save it. To do this,

Click ⊠ or choose File/Exit to close WordPad.

Choose: Yes

Creating a Shortcut Icon

Next you want to copy the Balloons file to your data disk in drive A. You could do this using the file icons shortcut menu and choosing the appropriate command. However, because you will frequently be using the A drive to access files, you decide to create a shortcut to the drive.

Concept 9: Shortcut Icons

A **shortcut icon** can be created for any programs, files, or other Windows features that you use frequently. If the shortcut is to a program, double-clicking the shortcut icon loads the program. If it is to a file, the shortcut loads the application the file was created in and opens the file at the same time. If it is to a feature, such as Windows Explorer, the icon shortcut displays the Explorer window. The shortcut saves you from having to select from menus or other icons in order to access the item. The shortcut icon contains a link to the appropriate application.

You will use the My Computer window to create this shortcut.

Open the My Computer window.

Select: [3½ Floppy (A:) icon]

Choose: File/Create Shortcut

A Shortcut dialog box appears, indicating a shortcut cannot be created in the My Computer window, and will be created on the desktop for you. Generally, shortcuts are created in the active window. If you wanted the shortcut icon in another location, you could simply drag it to where you wanted it to appear. However, you cannot add a shortcut to the My Computer window. Since you do want the shortcut on the desktop,

Choose: Yes

Your screen should be similar to Figure 3-22.

Figure 3-22

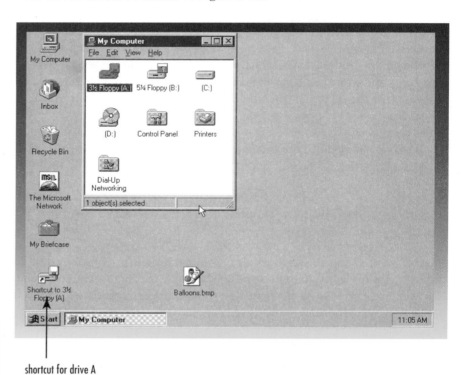

shortcut for drive A

> If you do not see the shortcut icon, it may be under the My Computer window. Move the window to see it.

> Click on the shortcut icon text box to rename the icon.

The shortcut icon is added to the desktop.
    Select the shortcut icon and rename it "A Drive."
    To see how the shortcut works,

Double-click:
        A Drive

The contents of your data disk are displayed in the A Drive window. This is the same as if you had selected the A drive icon from the My Computer window.
    Close the window.
    Now you can quickly copy the Balloons file to the disk in the A drive by dragging the file icon to the shortcut.
    Drag the Balloons file icon to the A Drive shortcut icon. The file is copied to your data disk.

Open the A Drive window and verify the file was copied to the disk in the drive. Close the A Drive window. Close the My Computer window.

Using the Recycle Bin

The Balloons file icon is still on the desktop. Since you have a copy of it on your data disk, you do not need the file on the desktop anymore.

Select:  **balloons.bmp**

To delete it from the desktop, you can use the Delete key, or you can drag the icon to the Recycle Bin icon.

Drag the Balloons icon to the Recycle Bin icon.

When a folder, file, or shortcut is deleted from the hard disk, it is moved to the Recycle Bin, where it is stored until you permanently delete it. This protects you from accidentally deleting files or folders that you might want later. When the Recycle Bin contains files, it appears full ; otherwise it appears empty .

To see the files that are in the Recycle Bin,

Double-click: **Recycle Bin**

Your screen should be similar to Figure 3-23.

deleted file in Recycle Bin

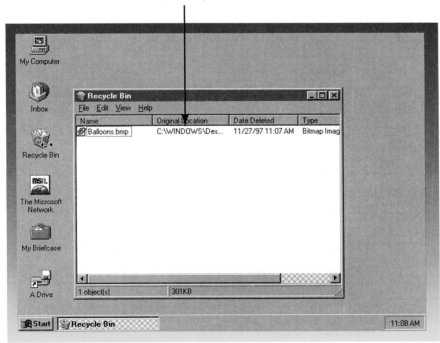

Figure 3-23

The Recycle Bin window is opened, and a button appears in the taskbar. To remove a file from the Recycle Bin, you would select the filename and press Delete or choose File/Delete. If you wanted to remove all the files from the Recycle Bin, you would use the File/Empty Recycle Bin command. You can also retrieve files from the Recycle Bin by dragging them back to the desktop or using File/Restore to return a file to its original location.

To remove the Balloons file,

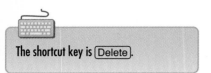

The shortcut key is Delete.

Select: **Balloons.bmp**
Choose: <u>F</u>ile/<u>D</u>elete

The Confirm Delete dialog box is displayed. This is another precaution against the accidental deletion of files you may want to keep.

Choose: <u>Y</u>es

The Balloons file is removed from the list. If you delete a shortcut icon, the shortcut is deleted, but the object to which it is linked is not deleted.

Close the Recycle Bin window.

Anything that is deleted from the hard disk appears in the Recycle Bin. The number of items the Recycle Bin can hold is determined by the size of the bin. This size is set to 10 percent of your hard disk space by default. When the bin is full, the oldest items in it are removed to make space for new items.

Using Quick View

After you have created a number of files and saved them to your disk, you may be unsure, with all the filenames which file you want to use. Instead of loading the program and opening the file, you can use the Quick View command on the File menu to check the contents of the file before launching the program.

You would like to find the file on your data disk that contains a resume, so that you can use some of the text as a guide to create a brief resume to send to a prospective employer.

Open the A Drive window (use the shortcut) and display the files on your floppy disk.

To view the file named Sample Resume before opening it,

> The Quick View option must be installed separately. See your instructor if this option is not available.

Select: **Sample Resume.wri**
Choose: <u>F</u>ile/<u>Q</u>uick View

The contents of a file containing a resume for Colleen T. Hayes is displayed in a View window. You can scroll through the document to determine if it is the file you want to open. This is the file you want to use. To open the document from the Quick View window,

> If Quick View is not available, double-click Sample Resume to open the file.

> The menu equivalent is <u>F</u>ile/<u>O</u>pen File for Editing.

Click: 🖹 **Open File for Editing**

Your screen should be similar to Figure 3-24.

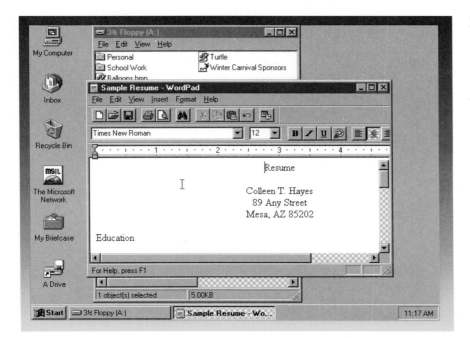

Figure 3-24

The Quick View window is closed, and the document is opened in WordPad.

Creating Scraps

You want to create a brief resume that will include some of the information in this file. The first sections you want to include in the brief resume are the resume header and the education section.

Select the text in the resume header and the entire education section.

You want to copy the selected text into another document. However, WordPad only allows you to have one document file open at a time. Rather than closing and opening WordPad documents, you will use the Windows 95 **scrap** feature. This feature copies selected text and places the copy in a separate "scrap" file on the desktop. The desktop must be visible when using this feature.

If necessary, restore or size the WordPad window so the desktop is visible.

Drag the selected text to the desktop.

Your screen should be similar to Figure 3-25.

scrap

Figure 3-25

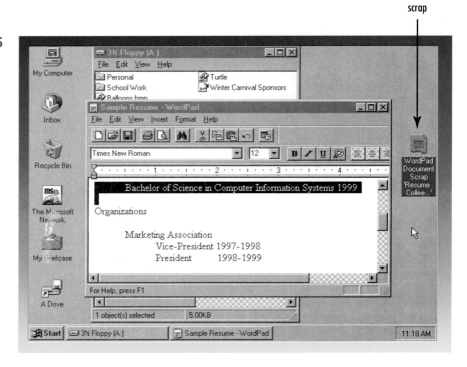

You can use the scrap feature only if your program supports drag-and-drop functions.

A WordPad document scrap is created. The default scrap name includes the application name and the first few words of the selected text in the document. A scrap can then be dragged to another document, where the contents are then pasted.

Next you would like to copy the information in the employment section of the resume to another scrap file.

Select the employment section and scrap it to the desktop.

You now have two scrap files on the desktop that you want to copy into the new document for the brief resume. To close the Sample Resume file and open a new blank document,

The command equivalent is File/New.

Click: [□] New

In the New dialog box, you are asked to specify the type of document to create and the name of the program to associate it with. The word processing program on your system is selected by default. To associate the file with the word processing program on your system,

Your instructor will provide you with the file extension if the file should be associated with a different program.

Choose: OK

A blank WordPad document is displayed. First you want to copy the contents of the scrap containing the resume header and education text into the document. To insert a scrap, you drag it to the document workspace where it will be inserted at the location of the insertion point.

Drag the [Resume...] scrap icon to the new document. If necessary, scroll to the top of the document.

Your screen should be similar to Figure 3-26.

scrap copied to new document

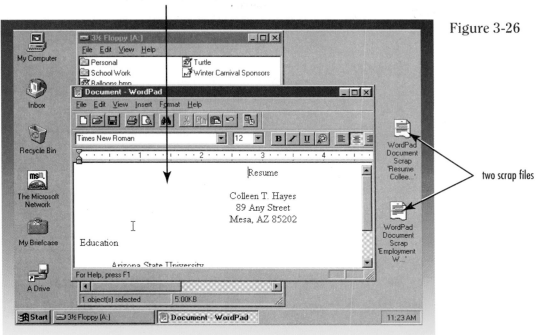

Figure 3-26

two scrap files

The text contained in the scrap file is copied into the new document. Notice that the formatting, in this case centered lines, is also included in the copy. Next, you want to copy the Employment scrap into the document. You want it to be placed above the Education section.

Move the insertion point to the blank line above the Education section. In a similar manner, copy the Employment scrap file into the new document above the Education section.

The document now contains the two sections from the original resume document.

Save the file with the name Brief Resume in the Spring 1998 folder of your data disk. Close WordPad. Close all the open windows.

You are returned to the desktop. Notice that the scraps are still displayed on the desktop. You can leave the scraps there, move them to a folder, or place them in the Recycle Bin.

Drag the scraps to the Recycle Bin. Drag the A drive shortcut to the Recycle Bin. Open the Recycle Bin and delete the two scrap files and the A drive shortcut.

Follow the procedure at your school to quit working in Windows 95.

> Select multiple files by holding down Ctrl while clicking each item.

LAB REVIEW

Key Terms

active character WN117	format bar WN116	server WN134
bitmap WN124	formatting WN118	shortcut icon WN141
compound document WN134	handles WN136	source file WN134
DDE WN134	linked object WN134	text box WN138
destination document WN134	object WN134	toolbox WN126
document WN114	OLE WN134	word processing WN114
drawing program WN124	points WN120	word wrap WN117
editing WN117	ruler WN116	workspace WN116
embedded object WN134	save WN122	
font size WN120	scrap WN145	

Command Summary

Command	Shortcut Key	Button	Action
Start Menu			
Programs			Displays folders and programs on your system
Programs/Accessories			Displays accessory programs on your system
My Computer			
File/Create Shortcut			Creates a shortcut icon
File/Quick View			Displays a preview of an unopened document
WordPad			
File/Save	Ctrl + S	🖫	Saves a file with same name
File/Save As			Saves a file with a new name
File/ Print	Ctrl + P	🖨	Prints the document
File/Print Preview		🔍	Displays document onscreen as it will appear when printed
File/Exit			Closes an application
Edit/Paste	Ctrl + V	📋	Inserts Clipboard contents
Edit/Paste Special			Inserts Clipboard contents as linked or embedded object
Edit/Select All	Ctrl + A		Selects all text in a document
Edit/Object			Activates linked or embedded object
Format/Font/Size		10 ▾	Changes height of characters
Format/Font/Color		🎨	Changes color of text characters
Format/Paragraph/Alignment		▤ ▤ ▤	Aligns text within margins

Command	Shortcut Key	Button	Action
Paint			
			Selects a free-form-shaped object
			Selects an object
			Erases part of drawing
			Fills an area with color
			Adds text to a drawing
			Creates a line
			Creates a polygon
			Creates an ellipse
File/E**x**it			Closes an application
Edit/**C**opy	Ctrl + C		Copies a selected object
Edit/**P**aste	Ctrl + V		Inserts contents of Clipboard
Recycle Bin			
File/Empty Recycle **B**in			Empties Recycle Bin of all files
File/**D**elete	Delete		Deletes selected item from Recycle Bin
File/**R**estore			Returns a selected item to its original location
Quick View			
File/**O**pen File for Editing			Opens viewed files in associated application

---

Matching

1. Match the following with the correct definition or function.

1) _____ **a.** adds a color to selected text

2) scrap _____ **b.** word-processing application

3) word wrap _____ **c.** displays a preview of document before it is opened

4) WordPad _____ **d.** undoes last action

5) _____ **e.** a drawing application

6) _____ **f.** centers text on a line

7) Paint _____ **g.** a file that is created when you drag part of a document to the desktop

8) _____ **h.** displays how document will appear when printed

9) Print Preview _____ **i.** moves text to next line when margin setting is reached

10) Quick View _____ **j.** adds text to a Paint document

2. Use the Figure below to match each action with its result.

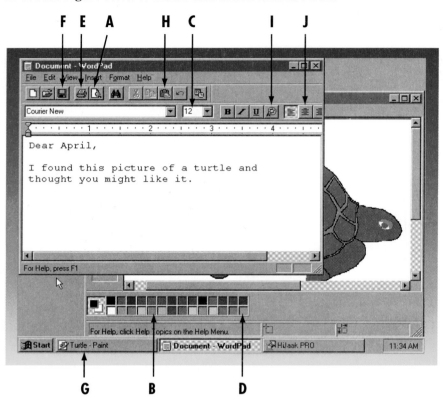

Action	**Result**
1. click C	_____ **a.** centers selected text
2. click I	_____ **b.** selects background color
3. click A	_____ **c.** selects foreground color
4. click H	_____ **d.** pastes text from Clipboard
5. click G	_____ **e.** makes window active
6. click B	_____ **f.** previews document
7. click J	_____ **g.** prints document
8. right-click D	_____ **h.** adds color to text
9. click E	_____ **i.** saves the document
10. click F	_____ **j.** changes type size

3. In the following screen, several items are identified by letters. Enter the correct term for each item in the space provided.

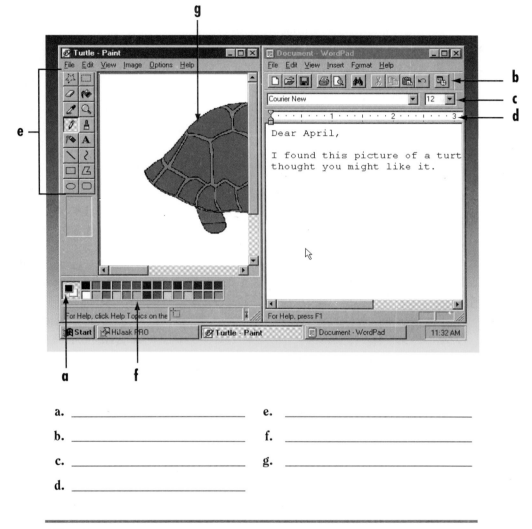

a. _____   e. _____

b. _____   f. _____

c. _____   g. _____

d. _____

Fill-In Questions

1. Complete the following statements by filling in the blanks with the correct terms.

   a. The _____ command can be used to preview the contents of a file before opening it.

   b. The bar containing shortcuts for many of the most frequently used menu commands is the _____.

   c. Paint is a _____ application and WordPad is a _____ application.

   d. As you type using a word processor, the _____ feature automatically moves text to the next line as it reaches the right margin.

e. A _____ can be created on the desktop for any program, file, or window feature that you use frequently.

f. The temporary storage area called the _____ holds cut or copied information until it is pasted or replaced.

g. _____ can be used to see the information that is stored in the Clipboard.

h. A graphic object that is selected and can be manipulated is surrounded by a box and eight solid squares called _____.

i. When a folder, file, or shortcut is deleted from the hard disk, it is moved to the _____.

j. A _____ file is created when you drag a selection from a document and place it on the desktop.

HANDS-ON PRACTICE EXERCISES

Step by Step

Rating System	☆	Easy
	☆☆	Moderate
	☆☆☆	Difficult

> You need the Windows 95 CD, or the Tour must be loaded on your system before you can complete this problem. Your instructor will provide you with instructions for loading the Tour of Windows 95.

☆

1. You will use the Tour of Windows 95 to complete this problem.

a. Load the Tour of Windows 95.

b. Choose Starting a Program from the Welcome to Windows 95 Tour.

c. As you read and work through the tour, answer the following questions:

1) What option on the Start menu is used to find a list of programs?

2) What can WordPad be used for?

d. Next, read and work through the Switching Windows tour until you can answer the following questions:

1) How can you switch to another open window?

2) How can you temporarily clear a window from the screen?

e. Exit the tour.

> Your instructor will provide you with the location of the file if you did not complete the previous lab.

2. While doing research for a history paper, you created the document History 1870. This file should be in the Fall 1997 subfolder in the School Work folder if you completed Lab 2.

a. Open the History 1870 document.

b. Select the text and increase the font size to 12 points.

c. Add the title "Rockefeller Controls Refining." Increase the font size of the title to 14 points and select a color of your choice. Center the title on the line.

   d. Enter two blank lines below the title.

   e. Enter your name below the paragraph.

   f. Preview and print the document.

   g. Save the document using the same filename.

3. As part of a graphic design workshop, you started to create a floor plan for a kitchen.

   a. Open the file Floor Plan on your data disk.

   b. Use the features you learned in the lab to modify the floor plan as shown below. Enter your name somewhere in the drawing.

Use Image/Flip to rotate the text.

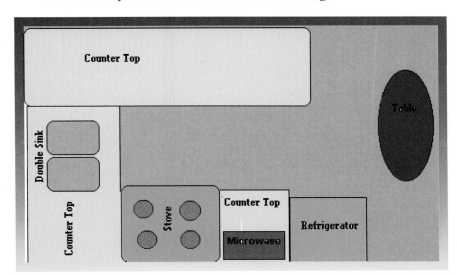

   c. Save your new floor plan using the same filename.

   d. Print the completed floor plan.

4. You are planning a children's birthday party and want to use Paint and WordPad to create a card for the party. To make a card that can be folded, you must place the picture upside down in the upper left portion of the page and the text in the lower right portion of the page.

   a. Open Paint and WordPad.

   b. Switch to the Paint application. Open the file Turtle.bmp on your data disk. Modify the colors of the turtle. Add any text that might be appropriate for the front of the card. Make the text 14 points.

   c. Flip the turtle graphic vertically. Rotate the text 180 degrees.

   d. Select the turtle graphic and text. Copy the selection to the Clipboard.

e. Embed the bitmap object into the WordPad document. Size the object until it is in the top left quarter of the page. Use Print Preview to check your layout.

f. Edit the embedded object to include a color box around the text.

g. Enter some blank lines below the graphic.

h. Below the graphic add appropriate text that would appear on the inside of the card. Include your name somewhere in the text. Size the text to 16 points. Righ-align all the lines of text.

i. Use Print Preview and adjust the layout of the document. (See the sample below for layout guidance.)

j. Save the document as Party Card. Print the card.

k. Fold the card so that the picture is on the front.

On Your Own

5. As the manager of Flowers and Bows floral shop, you would like to create a company logo. Use Paint to create a logo for the company. Copy the logo to a WordPad document and insert your name and the date into the file. Save the document as Flowers Logo. Preview and print the document.

6. Use Help to learn more about the Briefcase. Then answer the following questions:

a. If you want to work on files on your main computer and also on a portable computer, the Briefcase will _____.

b. To use Briefcase, you can _____ from shared folders on your main computer to the Briefcase icon on your portable computer.

c. When you are copying files from your main computer into Briefcase, the two computers must be connected, by a _____ or _____.

d. To automatically replace the unmodified files on your main computer with the modified files in your Briefcase, you would need to _____.

7. You can copy the contents of the active window or the entire screen using Windows 95.

a. For information about this feature, look up Screen Capture in Help.

b. Complete Practice Exercise 2 in Lab 2. Expand all the folders.

c. Capture an image of the entire screen. The screen is stored in the Clipboard.

d. View the Clipboard contents.

e. Paste the image in a blank WordPad document.

f. Size the object.

g. Capture a second image of the active window only and add it to the WordPad document. Size the image.

h. Enter your name and the current date in the document.

i. Save the document as Screen Capture. Print the document.

8. Disk cleanup: Do not complete this problem unless it is assigned to you by your instructor. You will not need any of the files or folders you used to complete this text. To clean up your data disk, remove all the folders from your data disk. You can now use the disk to hold other files you may need for the rest of this class.

Windows 95: Applications

Word Processor

Word processing applications are designed to help you create, edit, and print documents.

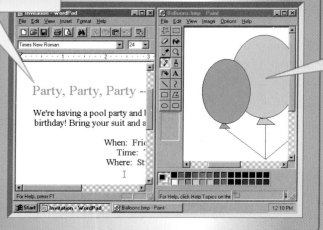

Drawing Programs

Drawing programs are used to create illustrations.

Concepts

Word Processor
Drawing Programs

Objects
Linking and Embedding

Editing
Selecting Text
Font Size

Saving Files

Shortcut Icons

Objects

An object is any set of information created in one application, then inserted or stored in a document that was created using a different application.

Linking and Embedding

When objects are copied from one application to another, they can be inserted into the receiving document as a pasted object, linked object, or an embedded object.

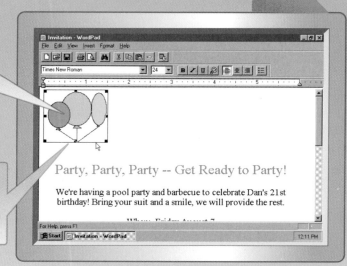

Font Size

Font size refers to the height of printed characters.

Selecting Text

Selecting highlights the text that will be affected by your next action.

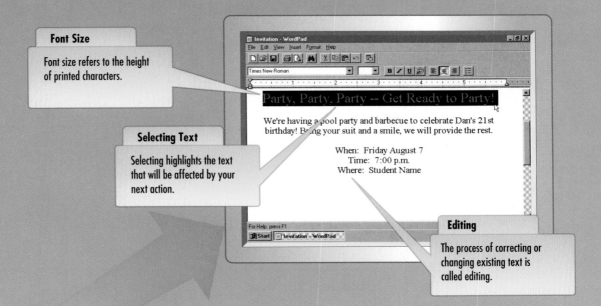

Editing

The process of correcting or changing existing text is called editing.

Saving Files

Saving creates a permanent copy of your onscreen document in a file on a disk.

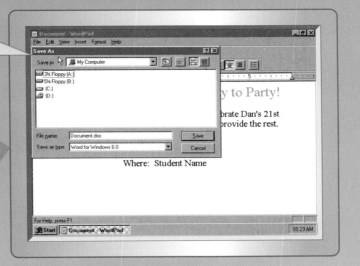

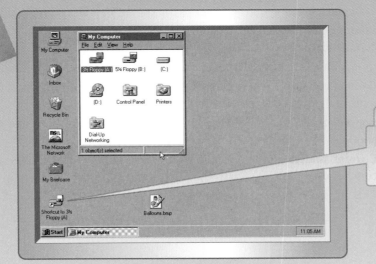

Shortcut Icons

Shortcut icons provide quick access to the associated feature.

WN157

Summary: Windows 95

Glossary of Key Terms

Active area: The area of the Exploring window that is affected by any action you perform.

Active character: The character after the insertion point.

Active window: The window you can work in. It is displayed in the foreground and the title bar is a different color or intensity to distinguish it from other open windows.

All Folders area: The left area of the Exploring window, which shows a graphic representation of the organization of the disk.

Associated file: A file that has a specific application program attached to it that will open when the file is opened.

Bitmap: Graphics that consist of arrangements of small dots.

Capacity: Refers to the maximum number of bytes a disk can hold.

Cascade: A window arrangement that layers open windows, displaying the active window fully and only the title bars of all other open windows behind it.

Choose: To select a command so that the associated action is performed.

Clipboard: An area of memory that temporarily stores and if necessary translates information to be copied or moved within or between files and applications.

Cold start: Turning on the power to the computer and starting Windows 95.

Common user interface: Programs that have common features, such as menu commands and toolbars.

Compound document: The document in which an object is inserted.

Contents area: The right area of the Explorer window, which displays the contents of the item that is selected in the All Folders area.

Copy: Feature that allows you to duplicate information from one location to another.

Current folder: The folder that your are working in and that is affected by commands.

Cut: To remove a selection and store it temporarily in the Clipboard.

DDE: Dynamic Data Exchange. The process that allows the linking of information between applications.

Description bar: The bar above each Explorer area that identifies the area's content.

Desktop: The opening Windows 95 screen used to display items on your screen in a similar way you might organize the work on your desk.

Destination: The location where you want to place a copy of the information stored in the Clipboard.

Destination document: The document in which an object is inserted.

Dialog box: A window that requests or provides information needed to complete a command.

Document: Any kind of text material such as memos, letters, and research papers.

Drag and drop: To copy or move a selected item by dragging it with the mouse to the new location.

Drawing program: An application software program used to create illustrations from line art.

Editing: The process of correcting or changing existing text.

Embedded object: An object that is stored in the destination document and can be edited using the server application.

Explorer: A Windows 95 application that helps you view and organize the files on your disk.

Extend a selection: To select more than one file at the same time.

File: The method of storing information on a disk. A disk can hold many files of different types.

Filename: A name assigned to a file. It can be up to 255 characters in length.

Filename extension: An extension of the filename. It can be up to three characters and is separated from the file name by a period. Generally, a file extension is used to identify the type of file.

Folder: A named division of the disk used to hold related files.

Font size: The height and width of printed characters.

Format: To convert a disk from its generic state into a format that can be used by your computer.

Format bar: The toolbar in WordPad that contains buttons representing the most frequently used text-editing and text-layout features.

Formatting: Enhancing the appearance of a document.

Graphical user interface: The capability to communicate with a computer by selecting graphic objects on the screen.

Handles: Eight solid squares displayed around a selected object, used to move and size the object.

Help: An application that provides information about commands and features.

Hierarchy: The tree-like representation of the organization of folders and files on a disk.

Icon: A graphic object that represents Windows elements, such as a program that can be run or a document that can be opened.

Insertion point: A solid blinking vertical line that is displayed in areas where you enter text. It shows you where the next character you type will appear.

Linked object: An object that is inserted into the destination document as a graphic representation of the data and is connected to the source document. Editing the source document changes the linked object.

Main folder: The top level of the hierarchy.

Maximize: To increase a window to its largest possible size.

Menu bar: The second line of a window, which displays the menu names that can be selected.

Minimize: To decrease a window to its smallest possible size.

Mouse: A hand-held hardware device that is attached to your computer. It controls an arrow, called a pointer, that appears on your screen.

Mouse pointer: An arrow-shaped symbol that appears on your screen if you have a mouse device installed. It is used to indicate items you want to select with the mouse. The pointer may change shape, depending on the task being performed.

Move: To remove information from its original location and insert it in a new location.

Notification area: Area in the taskbar to the left of the clock used to display indicators, such as a printer when printing is in progress or a speaker if the system includes audio hardware.

Object: An item in a window, or any set of information created in one application and inserted or stored in another application.

OLE: Object Linking and Embedding. The process that allows the creation of an embedded object.

Operating system: Program that controls computer system resources and coordinates the flow of data to and from the system unit and to and from input and output devices like the keyboard and the display screen. It allows you to create and manage files and run applications software programs.

Paste: To insert a copy the contents of the Clipboard into another location.

Pointing: To move the mouse pointer until the tip of the pointer rests on the item you want to choose.

Points: Font size measurement, with each point about $1/72$ inch. The larger the number of points, the larger the size of the characters.

Properties: Settings and attributes associated with an object. Most objects on the desktop have properties associated with them.

Pull-down menu: A menu bar command that displays a list of additional commands from which you can select.

Restore: To return a window to its previous size.

Ruler: A ruler, located above the document workspace in WordPad, that shows the line length in inches and the location of the margins and tabs.

Save: To store the work you have created using an application as a file on a disk.

Scrap: A file that is created when you drag selected text from a document and place it on the desktop.

Scroll arrows: Arrows in the scroll bar that move information in the direction of the arrows, allowing new information to be displayed in the space.

Scroll bar: A window element located on the right or bottom window border that lets you display text that is not currently visible in the window. It contains scroll arrows and a scroll box.

Scroll box: A box in the scroll bar that indicates your relative position within the area of available information. The box can be moved to a general location within the area of information by dragging it up or down the scroll bar.

Sector: A division of a disk track.

Select: To highlight a menu option or pick an item from a dialog box.

Selection cursor: The highlight bar in a menu.

Server: The application that created the embedded document.

Shortcut icon: An icon that provides a shortcut to any program, file, or other Windows feature that is used frequently.

Shortcut menu: A menu that appears when you right-click an item. It displays common commands associated with the selected item.

Source: The location that contains the information you want to cut or copy.

Source file: The document an object was created in.

Start button: A button in the taskbar that displays a menu of commands that are used to start a program, open a document, get help, find files, and change system settings.

Status bar: A bar of information displayed at the bottom of many windows. It advises you of the status of different program conditions and features as you use the program.

Subfolder: A folder that is created under another folder.

Tab dialog box: A dialog box that includes folder-like tabs that open to display related options. The tab names appear across the top of the dialog box and indicate the different categories of tabs.

Taskbar: A Windows 95 desktop element that contains the Start button, buttons representing active applications, the clock, and other indicators.

Text box: In a dialog box, an area where you type information needed. In a word processor, a user-created box that contains an insertion point and typed text.

Tile: A window arrangement that resizes open windows and arranges the windows vertically or horizontally on the desktop.

Title bar: The top line of a window or dialog box. It displays a name identifying the contents of the window or dialog box.

Toolbar: A bar of buttons commonly displayed below the menu bar that are shortcuts for many of the most common menu commands.

Toolbox: In Paint, the toolbar of buttons provided for many of the most common drawing commands.

Tooltip: A description that is displayed when you point to a toolbar or taskbar button.

Tracks: Concentric rings where data is stored on the disk.

Tree: The hierarchical organization of folders on the disk.

Unformatted: Disks that are shipped from the manufacturer in a blank form so that they can be used by a variety of computers.

Warm start: Restarting the computer without turning the power switch off and on again.

Window: A rectangular box that displays information in a dialog box and application programs on the Windows desktop.

Window border: The outside edge of a window.

Word processor: An application software program used to create text documents.

Word wrap: Word processing feature that wraps text to the beginning of a new line when the end of the line reaches the right margin.

Workspace: The large blank area in an application window where your work is displayed.

Summary of Selected Windows 95 Commands

Command	Shortcut Key	Button	Action
Start Menu			
<u>P</u>rograms			Displays folders and programs on your system
Documents			Opens files and related programs
Settings			Changes or views the computer system settings
Find			Locate files
<u>H</u>elp			Opens Windows Help program
Run			Starts a program using DOS command-line type functionality
Sh<u>u</u>t Down			Safely shuts downs your computer before you turn the power off
My Computer			
<u>F</u>ile/Ne<u>w</u>/<u>F</u>older			Creates a new folder
<u>F</u>ile/For<u>m</u>at			Sets up a disk for use
<u>F</u>ile/Create <u>S</u>hortcut			Creates a shortcut icon
<u>F</u>ile/<u>D</u>elete			Deletes selected item
<u>F</u>ile/Rena<u>m</u>e			Changes name of a folder or file
<u>F</u>ile/P<u>r</u>operties			Displays properties associated with selected object
<u>F</u>ile/<u>Q</u>uick View			Displays a preview of an unopened document.

Command	Shortcut Key	Button	Action
File/Se**n**d to			Copies selected folder and/or files directly to a disk
File/**C**lose		☒	Closes active window
Edit/**C**ut	Ctrl + X	✂	Removes selected object and copies it to Clipboard
Edit/**C**opy	Ctrl + C	🗐	Copies selected object to Clipboard
Edit/**P**aste	Ctrl + V	📋	Pastes selected object to new location
Edit/Select **A**ll	Ctrl + A		Selects all folders and/or files in active window

My Computer

Command	Shortcut Key	Button	Action
View/**T**oolbar			Turns on display of toolbar
View/Status **B**ar			Turns on/off display of status bar
View/Lar**g**e Icons		🔠	Displays folders and files as large icons
View/S**m**all Icons		⊟	Displays folders and files as small icons
View/**L**ist		☰	Displays folders and files as a list
View/**D**etails		▦	Displays all folder and file details
View/Arrange **I**cons/by **N**ame		Name	Organizes icons alphabetically by name
View/Arrange **I**cons/by **T**ype		Type	Organizes icons by type of files
View/Arrange **I**cons/by Si**z**e		Size	Organizes icons by size of files
View/Arrange **I**cons/by **D**ate		Modified	Organizes icons by last modification date of files

WordPad

Command	Shortcut Key	Button	Action
File/**S**ave	Ctrl + S	💾	Saves a file with same name
File/Save **A**s			Saves a file with a new name
File/ **P**rint	Ctrl + S	🖨	Prints the document
File/Print Pre**v**iew		🔍	Displays document onscreen as it will appear when printed
File/E**x**it			Closes an application
Edit/**P**aste	Ctrl + V	📋	Inserts Clipboard contents
Edit/Paste **S**pecial			Inserts Clipboard contents as linked or embedded object
Edit/Select **A**ll	Ctrl + A		Selects all text in a document

Command	Shortcut Key	Button	Action
Edit/**O**bject			Activates linked or embedded object
Format/**F**ont/**S**ize		10 ▾	Changes height of characters
Format/**F**ont/**C**olor		🖉	Changes color of text characters
Format/**P**aragraph/**A**lignment		▤ ▤ ▤	Aligns text within margins
Paint			
		⬭	Creates an ellipse
		◿	Erases part of drawing
		🖦	Fills an area with color
		▢	Selects an object
		A	Adds text to a drawing
		◺	Creates a polygon
		◥	Creates a line
File/Print Pre**v**iew		🔍	Displays document onscreen as it will appear when printed
File/**C**lose			Closes a window
File/E**x**it			Closes an application
Edit/**C**opy	Ctrl + C	🗐	Copies a selected object
Edit/**P**aste	Ctrl + V	🗒	Inserts contents of Clipboard
Recycle Bin			
File/Empty Recycle **B**in			Empties Recycle Bin of all files
File/**D**elete			Deletes selected item from Recycle Bin
File/**R**estore			Returns a selected item to its original location
Quick View			
File/**O**pen File for Editing		📝	Opens viewed files in associated application

INDEX

■ ■ ■ ■ ■ ■ ■ ■ ■ ■ ■